Getting It Right

Business Requirement Analysis Tools and Techniques

Getting It Right

Business Requirement Analysis Tools and Techniques

Kathleen B. Hass, PMP
Don J. Wessels, PMP
Kevin Brennan, PMP

MANAGEMENTCONCEPTS

MANAGEMENTCONCEPTS
8230 Leesburg Pike, Suite 800
Vienna, VA 22182
703.790.9595
Fax: 703.790.1371
www.managementconcepts.com

Printed in the United States of America

Library of Congress Cataloging-in-Publication Data
Hass, Kathleen B.
Getting it right : business requirement analysis tools and techniques / Kathleen B. Hass, Don J. Wessels, Kevin Brennan.
    p. cm. -- (Business analysis essential library)
ISBN-13: 978-1-56726-211-7
ISBN-10: 1-56726-211-2
    1. Business planning. 2. Business requirement analysis. 3. Industrial management.
            I. Wessels, Don J., 1945- II. Brennan, Kevin, 1972- III. Title.
            IV. Title: Business requirement analysis tools and techniques.
HD30.28.H3824 2008
658.4'01—dc22   2007021193

10   9   8   7   6   5   4   3

About the Authors

Kathleen B. Hass is the Project Management and Business Analysis Practice Leader for Management Concepts. Ms. Hass is a prominent presenter at industry conferences and is an author and lecturer in strategic project management and business analysis disciplines. Her expertise includes leading technology and software-intensive projects, building and leading strategic project teams, and conducting program management for large, complex engagements. Ms. Hass has more than 25 years of experience in project management and business analysis, including project portfolio management implementation, project office creation and management, business process reengineering, IT applications development and technology deployment, project management and business analysis training and mentoring, and requirements management. Ms. Hass has managed large, complex projects in the airline, telecommunications, retail, and manufacturing industries and in the U.S. federal government.

Ms. Hass' consulting experience includes engagements with multiple agencies within the federal government, such as USDA, USGS, NARA, and an agency within the intelligence community, as well as industry engagements at Colorado Springs Utilities, Toyota Financial Services, Toyota Motor Sales, the Salt Lake Organizing Committee for the 2002 Olympic Winter Games, Hilti US Inc., The SABRE Group, Sulzer Medica, and Qwest Communications. Client services have included maturity assessment, project quality and risk assessment, project launches, troubled project recovery, risk management, and implementation of program management offices and strategic planning and project portfolio management processes.

Ms. Hass earned a B.A. in business administration with summa cum laude honors from Western Connecticut University.

Don J. Wessels, PMP, is a Senior Consultant with Management Concepts, Project Management Division, headquartered in Vienna, Virginia. Mr. Wessels has over 25 years experience as a project management consultant, trainer, and public speaker. His areas of expertise include engineering, manufacturing, general business, and information systems and technology (IS&IT). His experience spans many commercial industries, such as banking, financial, professional services organizations, pharmaceutical, insurance, utilities, sales, and government organizations and has delivered many levels of project management training, from entry level through advanced and executive sessions. He facilitates project and program launches, conducts project management assessments, and assists clients in establishing project management methodologies and project management offices.

Kevin Brennan is the Vice President, Body of Knowledge, for the IIBA, the world's leading nonprofit association for business analysis professionals. He has a decade's worth of experience working as a business analyst and project manager in several different industries and is a regular speaker at conferences on topics including requirements analysis, business process management, and software quality assurance.

Table of Contents

Part III – Other Considerations

Preface

The Business Analysis Essential Library is a series of books that each cover a separate and distinct area of business analysis. The business analyst is the project member who ensures that there is a strong business focus for the projects that emerge as a result of the fierce, competitive nature and rapid rate of change of business today. Within both private industry and government agencies, the business analyst is becoming the central figure in leading major change initiatives. This library is designed to explain the emerging role of the business analyst and present contemporary business analysis practices (the what), supported by practical tools and techniques to enable the application of the practices (the how).

Current books in the series are:

+ *Professionalizing Business Analysis: Breaking the Cycle of Challenged Projects*

+ *The Business Analyst as Strategist: Translating Business Strategies into Valuable Solutions*

+ *Unearthing Business Requirements: Elicitation Tools and Techniques*

+ *Getting it Right: Business Requirement Analysis Tools and Techniques*

+ *The Art and Power of Facilitation: Running Powerful Meetings*

+ *From Analyst to Leader: Elevating the Role of the Business Analyst*

Check the Management Concepts website, www.management concepts.com/pubs, for updates to this series.

Part I

Preparing for Requirements Analysis and Specification

*T*his part navigates business analysts through everything they need to do before plunging into requirements analysis and specification.

Chapter 1 defines requirements analysis and specification.

Chapter 2 explains the infrastructure that must be present before requirements analysis and specification gets underway.

Chapter 3 addresses issues that are relevant when transitioning from elicitation to analysis.

Chapter 4 discusses requirements management, because you need to start thinking about managing requirements before you analyze and specify them.

Chapter 1

Introduction to Requirements Analysis

In This Chapter:

- Defining Requirements Analysis and Specification
- Challenges in Requirements Analysis
- Requirements Analysis Activities
- What Are Models?
- Stages of Requirements Analysis
- Wrapping Up Elicitation Before Starting Analysis

Defining Requirements Analysis and Specification

Requirements are the necessary and sufficient properties of a product that will satisfy the consumer's need. Software requirements are the necessary and sufficient properties of software that will ensure the solution achieves what it was designed to accomplish for its users and for the business.[1] Requirements for a new business solution, therefore, are the necessary and sufficient properties of a business system that will ensure the business goals and objectives are met.

Requirements analysis is the process of structuring requirements information into various categories, evaluating requirements for selected qualities, representing requirements in different forms, deriving detailed requirements from high-level requirements, and negotiating priorities. Requirements analysis also includes the activities needed to determine required function and performance characteristics, the context of implementation, stakeholder constraints and measures of effectiveness, and validation criteria. Throughout the analysis process, requirements are decomposed and captured in a variety of formats, in both text and graphics. Analysis represents the middle ground between requirements and design.[2]

Requirements analysis encompasses the activities involved in scrutinizing the information that has been elicited about the business need and the scope of a new or changed business solution. In analysis, requirements information is decomposed, examined, and restated until the requirements specifications are accurate, unambiguous, and complete. *Specifications* are representations of requirements in the form of diagrams and structured textual documents that are elaborated from and linked to the various requirement components, thereby providing a repository of requirements. Requirements analysis is an important part of the business solution life cycle (BSLC) process whereby business analysts, in collaboration with business and technical subject matter experts (SMEs), analyze and then specify, document, and validate the requirements of the business entity undergoing change (see Figure 1-1). Because the business analysis profession is just now emerging and a standard language has not been put into place, requirements analysis can also be referred to with any of the following phrases:

- Requirements engineering

- Systems analysis

- Requirements specification

- Business requirements analysis

In generally accepted engineering practice, requirements analysis and specification is typically completed before design and design is

Figure 1-1—Business Solution Life Cycle

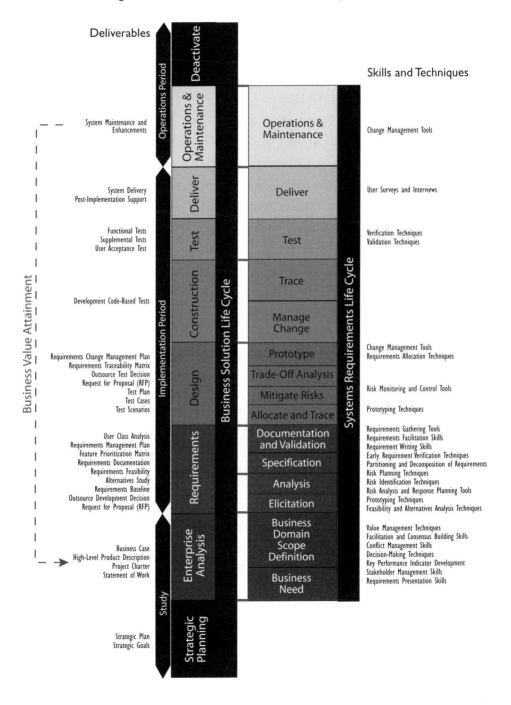

completed before construction. Of these phases, requirements analysis is considered by many the most vital part of the business solution development process. As mentioned in the first book of this series, studies reveal that project costs and technical risks can be reduced through rigorous and thorough requirements elicitation, analysis, specification, and validation. Indeed, it is not uncommon for projects that are following one of the agile methods for incremental development to spend up to nine months on requirements development and release planning prior to design and construction of the incremental releases. It must be noted, however, that requirements elicitation, analysis, and specification is an iterative process. Depending on the product development methodology used, it often continues at a progressively more detailed level throughout design and construction and even, to a limited degree, into the test activities.

The traditional way of doing requirements analysis is to capture all information about the business need in a single (often very large), rather unstructured document and leave the task of requirements analysis to the developers. However, organizations are beginning to realize that requirements analysis is a specialized field, with the analysis best carried out by experts. These experts are business analysts, who bridge the gap between the business world and the technology world. The business analyst's role is increasingly accepted in industry, as evidenced by the formation and rapid growth of the International Institute of Business Analysis (IIBA). (See the first book in the series for more information about the IIBA, or refer to its website, http://www.theiiba.org.) In addition, techniques used to analyze requirements are maturing into efficient and effective methods. Techniques introduced in the mid-1980s and 1990s, like a robust stakeholder analysis, the use of prototypes, Unified Modeling Language (UML), use cases, and agile development, are currently in vogue and promise to provide more effective analysis results than those of the past.

Challenges in Requirements Analysis

It is not a trivial endeavor to identify the relevant stakeholders, give them all an appropriate level of involvement in defining and validating requirements, and document their perspectives in a clear, concise format. In addition, the project team is expected to determine whether it is feasible to design and construct a new solution that meets the high-priority requirements within time, cost, legal, and ethical constraints. The challenges involved in requirements analysis are many, but they fall into three main categories:

- ✦ **People.** The right people—those with adequate experience, technical expertise, and communication skills—might not be available to lead and contribute to the requirements development activities.

- ✦ **Bias.** The initial ideas about what the solution should look like are often incomplete, optimistic, and firmly entrenched in the minds of the people leading the effort. Therefore, the requirements are constructed to meet the preconceived ideas.

- ✦ **Complexity.** The difficulty of using the complex tools and diverse methods associated with requirements analysis might get in the way.

Requirements Analysis Activities

The business analyst does not perform the requirements analysis activities alone, but instead performs them in a collaborative and iterative process involving key business and technical SMEs. Analysis activities include:

- ✦ *Modeling* requirements to restate and clarify them; modeling is accomplished at the appropriate usage, process, or detailed structural level.

+ *Studying* requirements feasibility to determine whether the requirement is viable technically, operationally, and economically.

+ *Trading off* requirements to determine the most feasible requirement alternatives.

+ *Assessing* requirements risks and constraints and modifying requirements to mitigate identified risks.

+ *Deriving* additional requirements as more is learned about the business need.

+ *Structuring* requirements into small, stand-alone, manageable components (usually feature-based building blocks) that can be implemented incrementally.

+ *Prioritizing* requirements to reflect the fact that not all requirements are of equal value to the business. Prioritizing is essential to determine the level of effort, budget, and time required to provide the highest-priority functionality first.

In addition, each unique requirement is assigned a set of attributes. *Attributes* are useful pieces of information about individual requirements that are used for a variety of purposes, including explanation, selection, allowing filtering and sorting, and validating.

As requirements analysis proceeds, *requirement specifications* are developed. Through this process of iterative, progressive elaboration, the requirements analysis team often detects areas that are not defined in sufficient detail, which unless addressed can lead to uncontrolled changes to requirements. *Requirements documents and models* are the output of the requirements analysis and specification process.

What Are Models?

Models are representations of components of a business process, system, or subject area, generally developed for understanding, analysis, improvement, and/or replacement of the process. Often, models are used to represent information, activities, relationships, and constraints that are relevant to the business area undergoing change. A model can take the form of a complex diagram, a structured document, a simple list, or a structured table. According to Ellen Gottesdiener, models are invaluable to business analysis because they: [3]

* Make the requirements development process more interesting and engaging to all stakeholders. Using both text and visual models provides variety and permits stakeholders to understand requirements from more than one perspective.

* Uncover missing, erroneous, vague, and conflicting requirements. Requirements models link together, allowing the team to discover related requirements and inconsistencies between models. Discovering and correcting these errors early results in higher quality requirements and reduces change and rework during design and construction of the solution.

* Tap into different modes of human thinking. Some people think more precisely with words, while others are better able to understand concepts with diagrams. Text representation of requirements is appropriate when a precise definition is needed, whereas visual representation is useful when depicting dependencies or sequence of events.

* Facilitate communication between the technical and business teams. Models let team members look at different aspects of the requirements from different perspectives.

It is importance to separate the modeling activities during requirements analysis from those performed during solution design. Analysis is concerned only with modeling the nature of the enterprise, and how it uses information to conduct its operations, whereas design is modeling the solution composed of technology (hardware and software) that supports any manual processes, policies, and procedures.

Requirements analysis is concerned with *what* is to be performed, not *how* it is performed. To complicate the issue even further, although modeling has been around for a long time, it is not widely practiced. This is not surprising, due to the complexity that abounds in the universe of models. Specific models are interpreted differently by different people and methodologies. Select any specific model, and you will find several alternative names, uses, and descriptions for it. The wise business analyst becomes expert at a few selected models that can be indispensable in documenting the business and validating business requirements.

Stages of Requirements Analysis

The three primary stages in the requirements analysis and specification processes, discussed in detail in Chapters 5, 6, and 7, are:

1. Analyze scope

2. Analyze requirements

3. Specify requirements for the new business solution

Wrapping Up Elicitation Before Starting Analysis

The elicitation phase must be at least partially complete before analysis can begin. In practice, the business analyst moves back and forth between elicitation and analysis. Partially complete means:

+ Interviews have been conducted with key stakeholders to discover their interests, success criteria, concerns, perspectives, etc. Interview notes should be drafted immediately following the interview.

+ Requirements elicitation workshops have been conducted, and the first iteration of several requirements models might have been developed, e.g., use cases, business rules, data models.

+ Several other elicitation activities have likely been completed, including focus groups, observation, user task analysis, and study of existing documentation. A summary of the activities that took place and the resulting learning has been prepared.

Chapter 3 of this book covers transitioning from elicitation. See *Unearthing Business Requirements: Elicitation Tools and Techniques*, a volume in the Business Analysis Essentials Library, for more information on requirements elicitation.

In addition, the following activities should be complete before analysis starts:

+ **Stakeholder identification and assessment.** At the start of the elicitation phase, an analysis of stakeholders was conducted. It should be reviewed and updated with information discovered during the elicitation. The stakeholders, or sources of requirements, are identified and assessed. New business solutions change the business environment and relationships between people, so it is important to identify all the stakeholders, take into account all of their needs, and ensure that they understand the implications of the changes brought about by the new business solution. To do this, a formal assessment of each stakeholder's level of importance to and influence on the project should be conducted. It is important to understand the degree to which the project cannot be considered successful if stakeholder needs, expectations, and issues are not addressed. Influence indicates the stakeholder's relative power over and within the project. A simple grid with importance on one axis and influence on the other is helpful. The scale could be low, medium, and high for each axis. The stakeholders in the high influence and high importance area should be considered key stakeholders. (See Appendix A, Stakeholder Analysis Template.)

♦ **Requirements planning.** The business analyst plans the requirements elicitation, analysis, specification, and validation activities in collaboration with the core project team members (the project manager, technical lead, and business lead) and documents the activities in the requirements management plan (RMP). The RMP was probably initiated at the start of elicitation, and it must be completed before analysis starts. At the same time, the core project team has begun to draft the project plan, schedule, and budget for the overall project. (See Appendix B, Requirements Management Plan Template.)

Endnotes

1.   Ellen Gottesdiener. *The Software Requirements Memory Jogger,* 2006. Salem, NH: GOAL/QPC.

2.   Scott Ambler. *Agile Analysis.* Online at http://www.agilemodeling.com/essays/agileAnalysis.htm (accessed April 2005).

3.   Ellen Gottesdiener. *The Software Requirements Memory Jogger,* 2006. Salem, NH: GOAL/QPC.

Chapter 2

Setting Up the Infrastructure

In This Chapter:

- Establishing the Requirements Analysis Team

- Selecting the Data Management and Requirements Archiving Approach

Infrastructure takes two main forms: setting up the analysis team and determining how you will manage and archive the requirements information. The requirements analysis team is typically an evolution of the elicitation team, and should be reconfigured and modified as needed. Before the requirements team can dive into analysis, the methodology and software that will be used for data management and requirements archiving must be chosen.

Establishing the Requirements Analysis Team

In the spirit of high-performing teams, business analysts align themselves with professional project managers, the best developers, and business visionaries to define business needs and determine the most appropriate, cost-effective, and innovative solution. Prior to beginning the analysis activities, the business analyst takes stock of the members of the requirements team that participated in the elicitation activities. To perform the analysis activities, additional experts might need to be brought onto the team, depending on the scope and complexity of the problem domain. However, the core team should be limited to six to eight members. To involve additional experts, establish subcommittees and plan for iterative reviews and feedback loops as often as necessary to mitigate requirements risks.

Organize for Success—The Core Team

It is incumbent upon the business analyst and the project manager to build an effective team. Early in the requirements analysis phase is an ideal time to build that outstanding core team. It is becoming clear that high-performing teams, whether in the military, sports, medicine, the arts, or business, have several things in common. Among them are:

- They are *small but mighty* (hence, the six-to-eight rule of thumb).

- They are *dedicated* to the project full-time.

- They are *highly trained and practiced*. Determine what training or practice activities might need to be completed prior to commencing requirements analysis activities.

- They are *coached*. Establish a team mentor or sponsor who is available in real time to solve any issues or remove barriers that might impede progress.

- They are *empowered*. Be sure that the core team members are respected, well versed in their relevant domains, and empowered to make decisions for their organizations.

- They are *multi-skilled*. Be sure that the members of your team have the appropriate skill set to complete the analysis activities. Team members should understand the business domain and the technical domain. They should also have experience in business modeling, requirements specification, stakeholder management, requirements validation, data management, and requirements management.

+ They have sufficient *tools and techniques* at their disposal. Ensure the team members understand the tools and techniques that will be used during the analysis process and are proficient in their use.

+ They have clear *roles and responsibilities*. Define and document team roles and responsibilities, as well as the team operating agreement. Continually revisit this document to ensure optimum team performance.

+ They have a *common vision*. When transitioning from elicitation to analysis activities, review the project documentation to date and ensure all team members understand and support the vision and mission of the project, including its alignment to organizational strategies.

+ They have *exceptional leadership*. Although the business analyst is the lead throughout the requirements analysis activities, she is wise to defer the leadership role to other team members when their expertise is required.

In addition, the requirements analysis team should be *colocated*. Establish a work room that will accommodate all core-requirements team members so that they can collaborate. Of course, some private office space might be needed as well, when team members are working on matters that require intense concentration.

Roles and Responsibilities

It is helpful to build a responsibility assignment matrix (RAM) for all those involved in the requirements effort. This matrix often accompanies a team operating agreement, which describes the basic ground rules the team will follow during the requirements development process. Refer to Figure 2-1 for a sample RAM.

Figure 2-1—Responsibility Assignment Matrix

Roles	Business Requirements Document
Business Owner	Initiator, Owner, Approver, Reviewer
Business Project Manager	Owner, Provider, Approver
Business User/SME	Provider, Reviewer
IT Project Manager	Owner, Provider, Approver
Business Analyst	Facilitator, Producer
QA Tester	Reviewer
Architect	Reviewer
IT Developers	Reviewer

Approver	Responsible for understanding information and agreeing to content through formal sign-off
Initiator	Drives the effort to organize necessary meetings and build consensus for completing deliverable
Facilitator	Ensures meetings are productive and professionally executed, ensures agenda is followed, and takes minutes
Owner	Responsible and accountable for the final results
Producer	Responsible for development and completion of deliverables
Provider	Provides information and subject matter expertise
Reviewer	Stays informed, is on the distribution chain, provides information and feedback

Selecting the Knowledge Management and Requirements Archiving Approach

The requirements need to be stored in an orderly fashion to allow ease of use and facilitate change management. Ideally, the data management approach was established prior to elicitation. In any case, it is essential that the documentation of existing and emerging requirements be stored properly prior to building additional requirements components during the analysis process, and that the requirements archiving and management process be well established, well understood, and well documented.

As data management procedures that are effective and well understood are developed, it is helpful to assign the primary responsibility for archiving and managing the requirements database to one person. If your project is large or complex, you might want to consider using a *requirements management tool,* which is a product that stores requirements information in a database; structures requirements for ease of use; captures all relevant information about requirements, including attributes and interdependencies; and assists in filtering and reporting requirements. Sophisticated tools integrate with configuration management and testing databases. An array of COTS requirements management tools are available.

The requirements management tool you pick should be based on the needs of your project and organization. Some tools cover the entire development environment and might dictate how you approach system development. The features and capabilities of any tool you are considering should be tested to ensure the tool will work with your development approach. Allow time for the learning curve, which can take up to a month. You should select the simplest tools that will meet your needs so as not to unduly bog down the requirements analysis process. The International Council on Systems Engineering (INCOSE) publishes a comparison of features of many requirements management tools on its website, http://www.incose. org. INCOSE updates the comparison periodically. The site also has a good discussion of the minimum capabilities of requirements management tools.

Chapter 3

Transitioning from Elicitation

In This Chapter:

- Review and Refine Existing Requirements Documentation

- Conduct Initial Requirements Risk Assessment

- Finalize the Requirements Artifacts to Be Produced

Looking at Figure 1-1, it appears as if requirements elicitation is completed before requirements analysis takes place. Elicitation, however, is very much an iterative process. The business analyst first collects information at a broad level, in an attempt to understand the scope of the endeavor. Next the analyst examines the information collected during the latest cycle of elicitation to uncover inconsistencies and oversights. The analyst then performs additional elicitation activities to progressively elaborate the requirements information. This iterative process can last from a week to a year or more, and it often continues throughout the BSLC.

Prior to plunging into requirements analysis, the business analyst examines the deliverables that were created during requirements elicitation. These may be in the form of interview notes, text requirements statements, the initial business requirements document, the first iteration of use cases, or even some rather sophisticated diagrams. After assessment of the current state of the requirements documentation, it is wise for the business analyst to conduct an initial risk assessment focused exclusively on requirements risks (discussed in detail later in this chapter). Identifying and managing requirements risks at this time goes a long way in preempting problems during analysis activities. Finally, the business analyst determines the requirements artifacts to be delivered at the end of the analysis activities. (See Figure 1-1, the Business Solution Life Cycle, earlier in the book.)

Review and Refine Existing Requirements Documentation

The core requirements team reviews all documentation that has been collected or developed during requirements elicitation from the various sources. The reviews are typically completed in a working session, walking through the documentation page by page, identifying any issues or ambiguities, and updating and refining the analysis plans accordingly. It is likely that the elicitation activities have produced high-level graphics and some text requirement statements. Likewise, if the elicitation activities did not allow time for stakeholder review and revisions based on the stakeholders' feedback, these steps are completed prior to formally beginning the analysis process. Conducting stakeholder reviews ensures that the requirements are accurate and complete. This stakeholder review and feedback loop is repeated throughout the analysis process to ensure that the members of the requirements team fully understand the requirements.

At this point, the project scope and requirements documentation is likely at a high level and ideally includes the following:

- Project business case, including or referencing any feasibility studies that might have been conducted before project launch (see the second book of this series for more information)

- Business architecture views, if available (see *The Business Analyst as Strategist: Translating Business Strategies into Valuable Solutions*, another volume of this series, for more information)

- □ Current-state models and documents

- □ Future-state models and documents

+ Project charter, including project selection and prioritization criteria and alignment to organizational strategies

+ Initial project plans and the requirements management plan (RMP), describing the activities to be conducted to elicit, analyze, specify, document, and validate requirements

+ Commitment to the funding and resources needed to complete the requirements activities

+ Stakeholder analysis matrix identifying the major stakeholders who will be impacted by or are involved in the project

+ Initial set of requirements documentation created during the elicitation workshops and interviews. This documentation represents the very first iteration of documented results of workshops and interviews, and it might include a simple set of written statements and notes. Depending on the rigor of the elicitation effort, requirements might also include a more robust set of artifacts, such as:

  - □ *Context diagram* (also called a *relationship map* or *domain model*). A context diagram depicts the scope of the organizational entity under study and shows the system boundaries, the external entities that interact with the system, and the major information paths between the entities and the system.

  - □ *Use cases.* A use case describes a series of steps an actor performs on a system to achieve a goal. Actors are objects of any type, such as people, parts, or other systems.

  - □ *Business scenarios.* A business scenario represents a significant business need or problem and enables understanding of the value of a potential new solution to the business. It describes a business process or application within the business and technology environment.

Conduct Initial Requirements Risk Assessment

Before commencing the requirements analysis activities, assessing requirement-related risks and identifying actions to avoid or minimize the high-probability and high-impact risks is prudent. If this step was completed prior to or during the requirements elicitation activities, now is an ideal time to revisit the risk mitigation strategy. Indeed, this requirements risk assessment should be revisited at key junctures throughout the project life cycle. In her book *The Software Requirements Memory Jogger,* Ellen Gottesdiener proposes the following steps to building a risk mitigation strategy:[1]

- Assemble the stakeholders to review and tailor the list of potential requirements risks (described below).

- Rank the risks according to *probability* (how likely the risk is to occur) and *impact* (how the risk will negatively affect the requirements process). A scale of low, medium, and high is typically used. For ease of discussion and classification, put some operational definitions into place. Doing so establishes sound criteria as to what *low, medium,* and *high* mean. The requirements team should discuss and arrive at a common understanding of these operational definitions.

- For high-probability and high-impact risks, identify ways to control, avoid, or mitigate the risks, and assign each risk to a team member to implement the actions to reduce the risk probability or impact and add the risk responses to the project schedule.

Requirements Risks Posed by the Business Stakeholders

In his book *Rapid Development*,[2] Steve McConnell provides a number of ways business stakeholders can hinder requirements elicitation and analysis activities:

+ Stakeholders do not know what they want.

+ Stakeholders are reluctant to commit to a set of written requirements.

+ Stakeholders insist on new requirements after the cost and schedule have been fixed.

+ Communication with stakeholders is difficult because of their competing demands.

+ Stakeholders do not participate in reviews.

+ Stakeholders are technically unsophisticated.

+ Stakeholders don't understand the development process.

These risks often result in requirements that are likely to change throughout the solution development process. The agile development movement argues that requirements will always change, not only because of the risks mentioned above but also because a business is a dynamic entity that is constantly changing. The obvious conclusion: the business analyst works with the development team to implement a solution development approach that embraces changes, reduces the cost of changes, and welcomes changes that add value to the business.

Requirements Risks Posed by the Technical Team

Typical problems caused by the solution development team include the following:

+ It is often difficult for the business and technical team members to communicate. The business analyst becomes the person who is bilingual, able to speak in both business and technical language. Often, it is the business analyst who analyzes and documents the business requirements and then works with a more technically oriented systems analyst to analyze and document the system requirements.

+ Analysis is often carried out by technically oriented staff members, rather than by business analysts with the skills and the domain knowledge needed to understand the current state of the business, the future vision, and what it will take to traverse from one to the other.

General Requirements Risks

Ellen Gottesdiener, in *The Software Requirements Memory Jogger*,[3] also presents a standard list of potential requirements risks. This is a good list to use with a group of stakeholders (business and technical) to begin to identify requirements risks:

+ Lack of user involvement

+ Unrealistic customer expectations

+ Developers adding unnecessary functionality

+ Constantly changing requirements (i.e., requirements creep)

+ Poor impact analysis when requirements change and evolve

+ Use of unfamiliar requirements techniques or tools

+ Unclear, ambiguous requirements

+ Conflicting requirements

+ Missing requirements

Finalize the List of Requirements Artifacts To Be Produced

Requirements artifacts, which are abstract representations of some aspect of the to-be-built system, take multiple forms. As previously mentioned, typical requirements artifacts include graphical models, structured models, tabular data, and structured or unstructured narratives and statements. A complete set of requirements documentation typically comprises diagrams, accompanied by explanatory tables, matrices, spreadsheets, and good old-fashioned requirements documents (all of these artifacts are commonly referred to as *models*). These artifacts, when organized and integrated into a useful set of information, provide essential details about the project scope, business requirements, and functional specifications.

Requirements must be clear and concise because they are used by virtually everyone in the project. In most cases, the verbiage used to document requirements should be natural, nontechnical language. A diagram can express structure and relationships more clearly than text. For precise definition of concepts, however, clearly articulated natural language is superior to diagrams. Therefore, representations in text and graphic form are essential for a complete set of requirements. Transforming graphic requirements into text can make them more understandable to nontechnical members of the team. This is one of the few times in the system life cycle that duplication is advisable.[4]

Of all the requirements artifacts, diagrammatic models are by far the most complex and the most specific to requirements, so a large portion of this book is devoted to models. So, what are models, and why do we need them? In the broadest sense, all requirements documentation, whether in text or diagram form, can be referred to as requirements models. There is an array of model types and uses. A model can be either a prototype (e.g., an early representation of a computer system screen or report) or an abstract representation of a complex component of the business solution (e.g., a data or process flow diagram). Models can be physical (e.g., an architectural model of urban design) or mathematical (e.g., a model depicting the interactions of many variables). Models can be used in simulations to relate various components, or they can be used as standalone tools to evaluate different approaches using different assumptions. Recent use of personal computers allows many types of software to effectively answer questions like "What if I increase the growth rate?" These, too, are models. Models can be used to depict a process, to investigate a known risk, or to evaluate an attribute of a business function. An engineering model is a technical demonstration model constructed to be tested in a simulated or actual field environment. Hardware and software models are constructed to prove or demonstrate technical feasibility. A mock-up model is a physical or virtual demonstration model, built to scale, used to verify proposed design fit, critical clearances, and operator interfaces.

In the case of *requirements understanding models* (the models we are primarily concerned with), diagrams are developed to demonstrate the understanding of a customer's problem or to help in figuring out what a business needs.[5] The purpose of models in the context of business solution development is to capture the business, data, and technology views in a graphical and text form. Visually displayed process and interface flows accompanied by text explanations vastly improve the comprehension of the scope and nature of the business requirements and facilitate design and development of the solution. Models also include the information that is essential to and complements the diagrams, such as documents, structured text, tables, matrices, and the like.

The requirements team attempts to select models that answer key questions—who, what, when, why, and how—to provide richer insight into requirements. According to Ellen Gottesdiener, some requirements understanding models are better suited to communicate requirements for certain business domains.[6] For example, transactional domains are well suited for *how* models (use cases and scenarios); structural domains are well suited for *what* models (data models); and dynamic domains are defined best by *why* models (business rules). Typically, the requirements team first develops models to define the scope of the change initiative and then goes on to describe high-level and more detailed-level characteristics of the business environment. We will briefly list the most used scope understanding and requirements understanding models here, and discuss some of them in detail in remaining chapters.

Scope-Understanding Models

Conventional requirement artifacts that define the scope of the business undergoing change and enhance understanding of business requirements are listed below. Although we don't think of these business artifacts as models, they are, in the sense that they are abstract representations of the business. More details and examples of these models are presented in the remaining chapters of this book. Typical models used to define the scope of the initiative may include:

- *Stakeholder identification and analysis matrices*, which list the individuals and groups involved in or affected by the new business solution and describe characteristics of each stakeholder, e.g., each stakeholder's role in the project and level of influence over project decisions. Refer to Figure 3-1 for a sample list of stakeholders.

- *Scoping diagrams*, which can take the form of context diagrams, scope diagrams, relationship maps, or domain models. These are types of reference diagrams that depict the scope of an organizational system in its environment, showing the system boundaries, the external entities that interact with the system (people and systems), and the major paths of information flow between the entities and the system.

- *Business vision, mission, strategies, goals, and policies* that have been documented and are in place.

Figure 3-1—Stakeholder Identification Tables

Stakeholders

The following tables identify the groups that are impacted by the project. Representatives from each of these groups participated in the scoping/requirements gathering discussions to help determine whether they needed to be involved in the project going forward and at what level.

Management Team

Stakeholder	Job Function/Impact
Mary F.	Business Sponsor
John S.	IT Sponsor
Sue B.	Business Owner
Marlene H.	Business Owner
Marty L.	IT Owner
Kathleen M.	Business Project Manager
Peter H.	IT Project Manager

Business Users

Stakeholder	Job Function/Impact
Paul H.	Business operations
Cathy J.	Underwriting
Allison L. Courtney G.	Mail operations
Susan G. Shelly K. Heidi L. John D.	Business analysis/User Acceptance Testing

Figure 3-1 (continued)

Information Technology

Stakeholder	Job Function/Impact
Marty L.	IT Development Director/Manager
Keith H.	Enterprise Architecture
Patrick O'M.	Quality Assurance
John K.	Infrastructure Group
Joe H.	Business Requirements QC

Vendor

Stakeholder	Job Function/Impact
Sean K.	Project Manager
Robert R.	Business Analyst
John D.	Business Analyst
Kent H.	Technical Lead
Les K.	Lead Architect
Chris K.	Technical Support
Walter L.	SME
David Y.	Chief Architect
Stan K.	Project Manager

Legal, Compliance, and Other

Stakeholder	Job Function/Impact
James Q.	Distribution
Alan K.	Systems and Hardware Asset Control
Dick S.	Accounting
Christy H.	Sarbanes-Oxley
Alice R.	Compliance
James S.	Legal
Collin H.	Internal Audit—Business
Alexis K.	Internal Audit—IT
Sarah W.	Information Security
Kathleen H.	Privacy
David H.	Finance—Service Delivery

- *Process flow diagrams* (also known as *process maps*), which are graphical representations of business processes.

- *In-scope lists* and *out-of-scope lists*, simple tools that help define specifics of the scope of the endeavor early in the analysis process.

Requirements-Understanding Models

Typical models used to understand high-level and detailed requirements for the initiative may include:

- *Data flow diagrams, data models, data dictionaries,* and *glossaries,* which depict and define the information needs of the business process.

- *Business rules,* which provide decision rules, calculations to be made, and event triggers.

- *Actor tables and maps,* which list the end users and other entities that interact with the business solution, their relationship to other users, and their roles and responsibilities.

- *Use cases, use case maps,* and *use case diagrams* using UML notation, which are techniques for describing the functionality of a business system horizontally, across business groups and entities. Each use case contains one or more scenarios that convey how the new solution should interact with a user (actor) to accomplish a business goal.

- *User interface diagrams, storyboards,* and *interface flow diagrams,* which describe how the actors interact with the system. These diagrams model the interactions business users have with the system that is contained in a single use case. At a high level, these models depict the overview of the user interface with the system, a combination of the interface views derived from all the use cases.

There is one more important activity that the business analyst performs prior to commencing the requirements analysis activities: preparing for requirements management, which is the topic of the next chapter.

Endnotes

1.   Ellen Gottesdiener. *The Software Requirements Memory Jogger*, 2006. Salem, NH: GOAL/QPC.

2.   Steve McConnell. *Rapid Development*, 1996. Redmond, WA: Microsoft Press.

3.   Ellen Gottesdiener. *The Software Requirements Memory Jogger*, 2006. Salem, NH: GOAL/QPC.

4.   Kathleen B. Hass. *The Business Analyst: The Pivotal IT Role of the Future*, 2006. Vienna, VA: Management Concepts, Inc.

5.   Hal Mooz, Kevin Forsberg, and Howard Cotterman. *Communicating Project Management*, 2001. Hoboken, NJ: John Wiley & Sons, Inc.

6.   Ellen Gottesdiener. *The Software Requirements Memory Jogger*, 2006. Salem, NH: GOAL/QPC.

Chapter 4

Preparing for Requirements Management

In This Chapter:

- Tailoring Requirements Artifacts to Your Project

- Communicating Requirements

- Tracing and Managing Requirements

- Capturing Lessons Learned

- Requirements Management Plan

Before the requirements team gets into the analysis process, requirements management issues must be carefully thought through. All too often, requirements teams struggle with managing the requirements artifacts *after* the requirements have been elicited, analyzed, and specified. Requirement information can become unmanageable if issues related to requirements management are not settled *before* getting too far into the requirements analysis and specification activities. In Chapter 2 we discussed the value of sophisticated requirements management tools. Suzanne and James Robertson, in their book *Mastering the Requirements Process*,[1] suggest making key decisions about the following additional requirements management issues early in the process:

- Tailoring the requirements artifacts to your project

+ Packaging the requirements artifacts for communication to different people and organizations

+ Tracing and managing requirements through the development of the solution

+ Seeking lessons learned and improving the process throughout the effort

The rest of this chapter explores these key issues that should be thought through prior to beginning analysis. Chapters 5, 6, and 7 explain the analysis process, and then Chapter 8 goes into more detail regarding the management of requirements after they have been analyzed.

Tailoring Requirements Artifacts to Your Project

The idea is to create only those models and conduct only those interviews and validation sessions that add value to the business or to the success of the project. The agile movement has taught us to use the motto "Barely sufficient is enough to move on." Ask the following questions about each requirement artifact to determine its value and, therefore, how detailed it must be:

+ Which current business models and documents need to be changed by the new business solution?

+ Who will use the artifact? For what will the artifact be used? Obviously, if there is no owner, or if there is no defined use for the artifact, omit it from your work plan.

+ When will the artifact be used in the project life cycle or ongoing operations?

+ Who will review and approve the artifact?

+ Who will produce and maintain the artifact?

Communicating Requirements

The requirements team drafts a communication plan to ensure that all key stakeholders are kept fully informed as the requirements emerge. The plan includes communication goals and strategies, stakeholder requirements, and the schedule of communication events. It is helpful to determine the publication mechanisms and methods at this early stage, so that the requirements artifacts will be documented and structured to facilitate communication. (See Appendix C, Communication Plan Template.)

The business requirements documentation template provides a mechanism for organizing and publishing all requirements information. (See Appendix D, Business Requirements Document Template.) However, other methods of communication, such as a management summary, a detailed statement of work to contractors, value-based information for marketing, and efficiency and usability information for end-users, might be more appropriate for selected stakeholders. The communication plan usually has two parts. The first is the team directory, followed by the information requirements for each team member listed in the directory.

Tracing and Managing Requirements

Who will be responsible for managing requirements? All too often, there is difficulty in effectively managing requirements after they have been documented. Prior to the analysis phase of the requirements process, the business analyst and project manager work collaboratively to define and implement processes and to ensure that resources are assigned to trace and manage the requirements. As the requirements emerge, they should be structured for ease of management at later stages. The following requirements management activities are described in more detail in Chapter 8, Requirements Management:

- *Allocating* (also referred to as partitioning) requirements to different subsystems or sub-components of the system. Top-level requirements are allocated to components defined in the system architecture, such as hardware, software, manual procedures and documentation, and training.

- *Tracing* requirements throughout system design, development, and testing to track where in the system each requirement is satisfied. As requirements are converted to *design documentation*, which is focused exclusively on the solution requirements (the *how*) instead of the business requirements (the *what*), the sets of requirements documentation, models, specifications, and designs are linked to ensure that the relevant business needs are satisfied.

- *Managing changes* and enhancements to the system. Managing requirements involves being able to add, delete, and modify requirements during all project phases. The challenge is to welcome change that adds value to the business solution and to continually seek ways to reduce the cost of changes. The accepted changes should stay within the objective and scope of the project. Or, if significant, the change might force a reexamination of the business value and strategy alignment of the project.

- *Validation and verification* of requirements throughout the project, facilitated by the business analyst. The purpose of verification and validation is to ensure that the system satisfies the requirements, as well as the specifications and conditions imposed on it by those requirements.

Capturing Lessons Learned

Lastly, at this juncture, ensure that lessons learned and feedback loop sessions are planned throughout the requirements analysis and specification process. Feedback and iteration are the best defense against requirements risks. The business analyst and project manager collaborate on these lessons learned sessions.

Requirements Management Plan

Virtually all the decisions that have been made during the activities discussed in the previous chapters should be captured in the form of a *requirements management plan (RMP)*, which is a subsidiary plan to the overall project plan and describes the activities, deliverables, and resource requirements for the requirements elicitation, analysis, specification, validation, and change management. Now that this plan is complete, we can begin the requirements analysis activities. The RMP is discussed in detail in another book in this series, *Unearthing Business Requirements: Elicitation Tools and Techniques*, and a template is provided in Appendix B of this book.

Endnote

1. Suzanne Robertson and James Robertson. *Mastering the Requirements Process*, 1999. Boston: Addison-Wesley.

Part II
The Analysis and Specification Process

*T*he following chapters discuss requirements analysis activities in detail. Chapter 5 presents the case for scope analysis and describes the most-often-used scope-understanding models.

Chapter 6 presents the case for requirements analysis and describes the most-often-used requirements-understanding models.

Finally, Chapter 7 describes the importance of structuring the requirements artifacts into an easy-to-use set of requirements specifications, and validating the requirements with both the business and technical stakeholders.

Chapter 5

Analyzing Scope

In This Chapter:

- The Case for Scope Analysis
- The Business Model
- The Context Diagram
- The Process Model
- Scaling the Models

We've covered all the preanalysis activities, and now we're ready for analysis itself. Recall that the three primary stages in the requirements analysis and specification processes are:

1. Analyze scope

2. Analyze requirements

3. Specify requirements for the new business solution

Since one of the main causes of project challenges is the failure to understand and manage the project scope, business analysis techniques are used to precisely define and visually depict the scope of the project. The scope of a business transformation initiative is multifaceted, and all of the facets must be fully understood:

+ **Project scope.** The work that must be performed to deliver a product, service, or results with the specified features and functions.[1] The project manager usually defines and manages this area of scope in collaboration with the business analyst and business and technical representatives.

+ **Product scope.** The features and functions that characterize a product, service, or result.[2] The business analyst usually defines and manages this area of scope in collaboration with the business and technical representatives. Several modeling techniques that are useful in defining the product scope are discussed in this chapter.

+ **Scope of business change.** The areas of the business that will be impacted by the implementation of the new product in terms of external and internal stakeholders, processes, functions, locations, and organizations. The business analyst usually defines and manages this area of scope in collaboration with the business representatives. Several modeling techniques that are useful in defining the scope of the business change are discussed in this chapter.

The business analyst plays the central role in the creation and management of scoping diagrams and text statements. Optimally, the business analyst helped to drive the scoping process during the preproject analysis activities and much of this analysis has been completed and approved. (See another book in this series, *The Business Analyst as Strategist: Translating Business Strategies into Valuable Solutions,* for more details about preproject business analysis, referred to as Enterprise Analysis.) Some of these scoping artifacts might have been produced during elicitation as well. (See *Unearthing Business Requirements: Elicitation Tools and Techniques,* the third book in this series for details about requirements elicitation.)

Either before the project is approved or during project start-up, the business analyst facilitates the scoping activities to help the project team define project objectives clearly, identify stakeholders, determine dependencies and risks, and document assumptions. The requirements team, led by the business analyst, documents the current state of the business processes and supporting systems, the reasons for the change, and the future state of the business processes and supporting systems the team would like to achieve as the end result of the project. The business analyst produces the scope-understanding models and manages the reviews, edits, and approvals required before the scope is finalized.

Once the project has been approved, there is a great deal of pressure to begin to dive into the detailed requirements. However, the business analyst attempts to keep the initial requirements analysis effort at a high level to grasp the extent of the change that will be brought about by the project outcomes. The purpose of this high-level analysis is to ensure that everyone involved in the project understands the scope of the endeavor. It is imperative to describe the effort at a high level before defining the details because otherwise the scope is likely to be poorly understood, the project time and cost are likely to be underestimated—and, consequently, underfunded—and the effort can quickly spiral into a failed or challenged project. Therefore, if high-level analysis models were not created during prior periods of the project, they are developed at this point.

The Case for Scope Analysis

Despite the emphasis on project management best practices over the past decade, many organizations still operate in an immature, ad hoc manner that usually results in a rush to develop the solution before the business need is understood. Indeed, some organizations use the emerging agile project management approach as an excuse for not eliciting, analyzing, and specifying requirements in a disciplined manner. In practice, an immature, ad hoc approach is often viewed as a necessary evil by organizations that have many high-profile projects with tight deadlines. A thorough requirements effort is considered a luxury.

Many project teams just dive in without a clear understanding of their overall organization. Misalignment with the organizational strategies, goals, and mission often takes a project off course. This inability to understand the business then permeates every aspect of the project. Many project sponsors and their respective management teams have a silo or stovepipe vision of their organization and how it interacts within the enterprise. Consequently, many affected stakeholders are not identified, resulting in development of a new business solution that does not meet the business needs in total.

Creating a model or architectural view of the business as it operates today (the current-state or as-is model) fosters understanding of the components of the business under study. Depicting the current view of the business is a crucial first step in the process of analyzing requirements for changes to the current state. The requirements team then creates the future-state or to-be model of the business—how it will look after the new business solution is deployed. The difference between the current and future states, referred to as the *gap*, represents the amount of change required. These as-is and to-be models are invaluable in scoping, analyzing, and defining the business requirements for significant changes to the business.

The Business Model

Figuring out the business requirements is very difficult if the requirements team does not understand the business as a whole entity. As discussed in *The Business Analyst as Strategist: Translating Business Strategies into Valuable Solutions*, another volume in this series, creating and maintaining the business architecture using business modeling techniques is an extremely valuable process. To quote Ellen Gottesdiener, "business modeling helps you understand how the results of the project will support the business processes."[3] The purpose of business modeling is to:

- Understand the structure and the dynamics of the existing organization.

- Ensure that all stakeholders, customers, end users, and team members have a common understanding of the organization.

- Discern how to deploy new systems and products to facilitate business operations and add business value.

- Discover which existing systems and organizations might be affected by the results of the project.

Developing the business architecture, which comprises models in the form of documents, graphs, and other descriptive information about the business, is an arduous undertaking. Although many organizations have not made the effort to architect their business, it is becoming clear that describing the current and future states of the business is an essential practice to help manage the complexity in business entities today. Because modeling the business as a whole often takes more time and effort than an organization is able to support, it is important to scale the modeling activities to fit the needs of the project.

In most organizations, the current- and future-state business architecture models either do not exist or are complete for only a particular group within the enterprise. If models of the business component(s) under consideration do exist, the business analyst conducts a thorough examination of the models with the affected stakeholders. Given the size, complexity, and risk of the project, the stakeholders should validate that the models are accurate and complete in enough detail to serve the needs of the project.

If current-state models of the business area under consideration do not exist, the business analyst and requirements team address this need first. The business modeling effort requires executive sponsorship because of the need for a considerable amount of customer involvement. If the project requires significant business process and organizational change, potentially involving regulatory and legal issues, future-state models will become an essential component of the requirements package. Business representatives need to be enlisted to help define new organization structures, processes, policies, procedures, business rules, and other business documentation, as well as to communicate and manage the change. Business modeling helps identify where the major organizational and cultural changes will be required so they can be addressed early. If the significant organizational issues are not addressed properly, there is a good chance that implementation of the new solution will not be optimal, thus putting the expected business value at risk.

Two models are recommended to quickly architect the business: the *context diagram* and the *process map*. Both should be created, because context diagrams provide a view of the boundaries of the change initiative and the process map depicts the business processes undergoing change. They are discussed in detail in the remainder of this chapter. To complement these two business models, the business analyst collects, reviews, and brings current, or develops if nonexistent, the basic information that typically exists about the business entity undergoing change. The business analyst may update these artifacts as required by the requirements of the project. This information may include:

+ Business mission, strategy, goals, and measures of the enterprise.

+ Goals and objectives by line of business (LOB) and/or business unit under consideration.

+ Business functions description accompanied by decomposition of major functional areas, by LOB and/or business unit.

+ Business products and services by LOB and/or business unit.

+ Organization structure including LOBs, business units, service centers, distribution center, etc., and their locations.

+ Business processes, including measures and deliverables by LOB and/or business unit.

+ Business roles, including knowledge and skill requirements by LOB and/or business unit.

+ Legal or regulatory constraints by LOB and/or business unit.

+ Business rules that impose constraints on the business by LOB and/or business unit.

+ Stakeholder list that was created during early project planning and captured in the project management plan. The business analyst reviews and refines the list to encompass all key stakeholders that will be involved in the requirements analysis activities. Refer back to Figure 3-1, Stakeholder Identification Tables.

+ In-scope/out-of-scope list that is often created during early project planning and captured in the project management plan. The business analyst reviews and refines the list to encompass all in-scope/out-of-scope areas identified to date. Refer to Figure 5-1 for a sample in-scope/out-of-scope list.

We will now discuss the two key diagrams used to define project scope. It is important to note that the purpose of this book is not to get into the details of how to create the various models, which is a lengthy and complex process. There are many excellent resources for step-by-step instructions for creating models, including *The Software Requirements Memory Jogger* by Ellen Gottesdiener.

Figure 5-1—In-Scope and Out-of-Scope List

In Scope

- Implement a workflow system in 1Q2007

- Business areas:
  - All life and annuity claims
  - All life and annuity call centers

- Functionality:
  - Scanning and indexing
  - Routing, prioritization, and management
  - Forms management
  - Archive and retrieval
  - Fax
  - E-mail
  - Mailroom
  - Records management

- Non-functional requirements:
  - User access
  - Service levels
  - Legal, SOX, and privacy
  - Internal audit
  - Security

- Process redesign

- Conversion of existing information

- As-is (current state) and to-be (future state) process flows

- Business, functional, and non-functional requirements

Figure 5-1 (continued)

+ Test plan

+ Hardware sizing and cost estimates

+ Infrastructure design

Out of Scope

The following is currently out of scope for Phase 1 of project:

+ Business areas:
  - Group pensions
  - Immediate annuities
  - Reinsurance
  - Controllers
  - Concierge
  - International service

+ Functionality:
  - Bar coding and forms redesign
  - Optical character recognition
  - Scanning and conversion of existing forms
  - Work tracking history data conversion
  - Outgoing mail and statements
  - Mail operations

+ Automated lockbox feeds

+ Call tracking database

+ Planning, analysis, requirements, or estimation for hardware sizing

+ Analysis, plan, or requirements for operations center

+ Detail design activities that have no impact on the system

The Context Diagram

A *context diagram* is a graphical illustration showing what information and products are exchanged among external customers, providers, and key functions in the organizational component undergoing review. It is also known as an *organizational context diagram, problem domain model,* or *relationship map.*

The context diagram is a behavioral model and is orientated toward processes, tasks, and sequences. It answers the question, "What is going to happen when this process is executed?" It is particularly useful when you are answering questions about who or what parts of your organization are involved and what external customers and suppliers provide. The inputs and outputs depicted represent high-level information about the interactions that exist within the organizational component. The context diagram helps to identify opportunities to design changes to business processes to increase efficiencies, reduce costs, or add value in other ways. In addition, analysis of the relationships often uncovers redundancies, repetition, multiple external interfaces, and missing inputs or outputs.

In the context diagram, rectangles represent each entity and arrows between the rectangles represent function inputs and outputs that go across entities. The diagram may also depict function arrows within a rectangle. Refer to Figure 5-2 for an example of a context diagram for obtaining customer information.

The Process Model

A *process model* is a graphical representation of a business process. It takes on many forms. Types of process models are known as *swim lane diagrams, workflow maps, process maps, activity diagrams, line of visibility models,* or *cross-functional process maps.* The process model depicts the sequence of steps, the flows of inputs and outputs across functions, business components, or job roles for a specific work process. Process models are especially useful when identifying what organizational processes and organizational structural changes

Figure 5-2—Context Diagram for Obtaining Customer Information

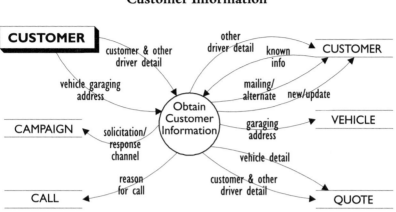

might be necessary as a new business solution is implemented. On this diagram:

+ Horizontal lanes represent the functions or roles.

+ Boxes represent the steps in the process.

+ Diamonds represent the decisions.

+ Arrows show the flow of the work.

A process model is particularly useful when you are asking questions such as:

+ How does it work?

+ What decisions are made along the way?

+ Who makes the decisions?

Assuming business process models exist, the business analyst facilitates meetings with SMEs to review the current-state business process models and identify where improvements might be made—

or must be made to accomplish the project objectives. Improvements can range from incremental changes to complete redesign of the process. During the working sessions, the business analyst uses his or her expertise to analyze existing business process models and recommends process improvements. Upon completion of the future-state business process models, the process is captured using Visio or other flowcharting software. The diagrams include the proposed business processes, the activities being undertaken, who undertakes the activities, and the systems and tools to be used to support the business process. Written explanations of each step and process are included to provide the details. Once the current-state and proposed future-state business process documentation is complete, it is reviewed and approved by the project team and impacted stakeholders. Refer to Figure 5-3, which depicts a generic process model with swim lanes depicting the person, team, or business area that owns the activities contained within the lane.

Although there are different notation choices for process models, such models share similar characteristics. They:

+ Indicate process flows

+ Focus on handoffs

+ Show system or organizational responsibilities

Scaling the Models

An understanding of the current and future states of the business starts to emerge with the creation of context diagrams and process flow maps. The idea here is to get a high-level view, but how high is high enough? This early view is often at the very highest level, depicting a simple, broad-based understanding of the organizational component. The view may be the "30,000 feet from an airplane" view, or business models might need to take the form of a more detailed look at a business entity, perhaps at the division or department level.

Figure 5-3—Requirements Management and Development Process Model

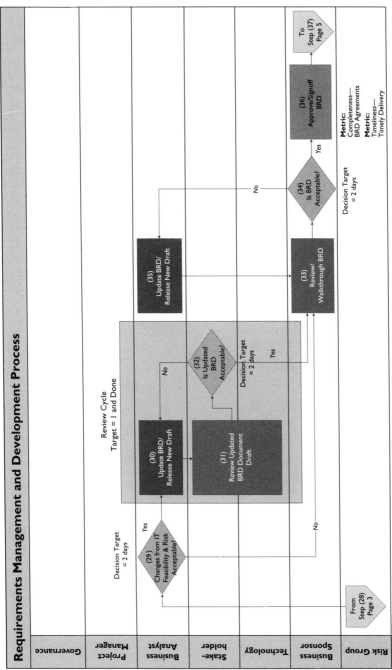

This might be more of a 10,000-foot or mid-level view. The 1,000-foot level is an even more detailed view.

The business analyst works with the core requirements team to scale the business models to meet the needs of the project. The guideline is to develop just enough detail to move on—no more, no less. Over time, as each new project comes online, the business models facilitate understanding of the current state of the business for which the project was undertaken. The creation or update of the business models provides a baseline of the business process. The more business architecture modeling conducted in an organization that is managing complex change, the more likely its projects will succeed.

Endnotes

1. Project Management Institute. *A Guide to the Project Management Body of Knowledge,* 3rd ed., 2004. Newtown Square, PA: Project Management Institute, Inc.

2. ibid.

3. Ellen Gottesdiener. *The Software Requirements Memory Jogger,* 2006. Salem, NH: GOAL/QPC.

Chapter 6

Analyzing Requirements

In This Chapter:

- An Overview of Requirements Analysis
- Requirements Understanding Models
- Selecting the Appropriate Models

The requirements analysis effort is the second of the three primary stages in the requirements analysis and specification processes, coming after scope analysis (covered in Chapter 5) and before requirements specification (covered in Chapter 7). The business analyst plays the central role in the requirements analysis process, collaborating with key members of the team.

It is widely believed that the leading cause of failed and challenged projects is the gap between what the business team needs and what the technical team understands and delivers. To address this issue, the era of the business analyst's drafting a requirements document and passing it over the wall to the development team is over. Traditional requirements documents are difficult to translate into designs because they are not usually structured as a narrative of what the new business solution must do. The new, contemporary approach to requirements analysis is designed to bridge the gap by taking the requirement information gathered during elicitation, analyzing it, and specifying the requirements in a structured, business-focused manner.

An Overview of Requirements Analysis

Requirements analysis is the process of structuring requirements information into various categories, evaluating requirements for selected qualities, representing requirements in different forms, and deriving detailed requirements from high-level requirements. Figure 6-1 shows where requirements analysis falls in the BSLC.

Requirements analysis is about creating a *guidebook* for an effort to build a new business system. It involves stating requirements in multiple ways so that:

+ They are sufficiently understood by all stakeholders.

+ Needs can be prioritized by the customer.

+ Developers can design and build the optimum solution.

As we get better at using sophisticated analysis tools and techniques, requirements analysis is becoming essentially an *architectural* endeavor, translating a set of business views of the enterprise into comprehensive architectural diagrams and supporting documentation. An *architecture* is defined as "a unifying or coherent form or structure." A critical mission of the business analysis profession, therefore, is to translate the business requirements information discovered during elicitation into a coherent form or structure. Since

Figure 6-1—Where Analysis Falls in the BSLC

Elicitation	Analysis	Specification	Documentation and Validation

business systems are essentially invisible, the effort to create the business architecture makes the enterprise *able to be seen.*

Most requirements analysis experts restrict analysis to focus on *what* is to be done, not *how* to do it. Therefore, the models produced during analysis are *solution-independent* and *technology-neutral*, i.e., analysis models describe the business without regard for the solution that might be built to address the business need. This approach frees the designers from constraints, allowing them to come up with solution options without preconceived ideas.

Requirements analysis is primarily the responsibility of the business analyst, but it is performed collaboratively with members of the core project team. During the analysis process, we attempt to answer the following questions:

- What are the scope and objective of the effort? (discussed in the previous chapter)

- What does the enterprise look like? What are its components in terms of:

  □ Vision, mission, strategies, measures of success

  □ Business processes, policies, procedures, activities, events, triggers, timing

  □ Organizations, people, roles, competencies

  □ Locations of business units

  □ Data and information

  □ Application systems

  □ Technology infrastructure

- How much change will be needed in the enterprise to achieve the objective?

The outcomes of the analysis process are *analysis models*, business requirements represented by a combination of diagrams and structured text, such as lists, tables, or matrices. Analysis models supplement the requirements specified in the *business requirements document*, which is written in natural language using declarative statements (and is discussed more fully in the next chapter). As covered in the next chapter, after the requirements are well organized, specified, and structured, the requirements team prioritizes the requirements by analyzing trade-offs among the requirements in terms of value added to the business versus technical risk and complexity.

Requirements-Understanding Models

It is incumbent upon the business analyst to engage the business sponsor, users, and customers to gain a clear view of the ultimate objectives of the project and to define a successful outcome in business terms. In the previous chapter, we discussed the need to analyze scope by modeling the business at a high level. Business stakeholders are vital at this point so that the requirements team understands the business drivers (e.g., sell more products at a reduced cost of doing business through web-enabled order entry, expand the high-end customer base through acquisition). The process of analyzing scope should be completed quickly, taking days not weeks. The goal is to understand the objectives and scope of the project, not to get to the details.

Continuing the analysis process, the team next begins to drive down to the details by creating artifacts that describe the fundamental structures and concepts that compose the business entity, thus developing an architectural view of the part of the enterprise undergoing change. The business analyst actually *translates* the business view into an architectural view. Only then can the business validate the quality of the translation and use the architectural view as a vehicle of communication between the business and the technical community.

Because business systems are complex, business analysts not only must understand how to apply a wide range of modeling tools and techniques but also must select the appropriate models for each specific project. Table 6-1 presents an adaptation of Scott Ambler's list of a wide variety of models that may be used to analyze requirements or, later, to design the solution. Ambler indicates whether the technique is simple enough for stakeholders to learn, whether it is usually a paper-based artifact, whether he would suggest creating it on a whiteboard, and what type of software he would consider using to create and maintain it.[1] Use this table to gain an understanding of the universe of modeling artifacts that have emerged in the business analysis world.

Table 6-1—Potential Requirements-Understanding Models

Modeling Artifact	Simple	Paper	White-board	Software
Test plans				FITNesse or similar test management tool
Business rules		Card		Word processor
Constraints		Card		Word processor
Data flow diagram (DFD)			X	CASE tool
User interface prototype	X	Flip chart		
Features	X	Card		Spreadsheet
Free-form diagrams	X		X	Diagramming tool
Process flowcharts			X	Diagramming or CASE tool
Glossary		Card		Word processor
Data models				CASE tool
Network diagram				Diagramming tool
Robustness diagram			X	Diagramming tool
Security model			X	Diagramming tool
UML 2 activity diagram			X	CASE tool
UML 2 class diagram			X	CASE tool
UML 2 communication/ collaboration diagram			X	Diagramming tool

Table 6-1—Potential Requirements-Understanding Models (continued)

Modeling Artifact	Simple	Paper	White-board	Software
UML 2 component diagram			X	CASE tool
UML 2 composite structure diagram			X	Diagramming tool
UML 2 deployment diagram			X	CASE tool
UML 2 interaction overview diagram			X	Diagramming tool
UML 2 object diagram			X	Diagramming tool
UML 2 package diagram			X	CASE tool
UML 2 sequence diagram			X	CASE tool
UML 2 state machine diagram			X	CASE tool
UML 2 timing diagram			X	CASE tool
UML 2 use case diagram			X	CASE tool
Usage scenario	X	Card		Word processor
User interface flow diagram (storyboard)			X	Diagramming tool
User interface prototype			X	Prototyping tool or IDE
User story	X	Card		Spreadsheet
Value stream map			X	Diagramming tool

The business analyst must also determine what types of text models (documents/specifications) need to be created to accompany the graphical models. Even when using the most lean methodology, some documentation is required. Table 6-2 presents a list of the most common documents that the business analyst creates as part of the final requirements package. This list was adapted from Scott Ambler's comprehensive list of all potential project documentation.[2] The next chapter presents a detailed discussion of the specification documents.

Table 6-2—Potential Specification Documents

Document	Audience	Description	Advice
Business case and executive briefings	Senior management, user management, project management	A definition of the vision for the system and a summary of the current cost estimates, predicted benefits, risks, staffing estimates, and scheduled milestones.	This document is typically used to gain funding and support for your project, as well as to provide status updates to important project stakeholders that might not be actively involved with your project on a day-to-day basis.
Requirements specification documents	All stakeholders	Documents that define what the system will do, summarizing requirements such as functional requirements, supplemental requirements, business rule definitions, use cases, user stories, or essential user interface prototypes (to name a few).	Agile projects typically favor inclusive requirements techniques such as user stories. Projects using traditional methods tend toward more formal requirements artifacts and documentation such as: • User requirements document • Business requirements document • Use cases • System requirements document • Concept of operations (ConOps) • Requirements definition document • Software requirements document • System definition document • Functional specification • Supplemental specification • Technical specification • Product specification
User documentation	Users, user managers	The end-users often require a reference manual, a usage guide, a support guide, and training materials.	If use cases have been developed, base the usage guide and training materials on the use cases for the system. The use cases describe how the actors work with the system, and therefore they should be a very good foundation on which to base both of these documents.

Because the goal is to understand the requirements (not just to create requirements documentation), the sophisticated business analyst drafts only those documents and creates only those models that will add value to the project in terms of understanding and validating the business requirements. Likewise, when writing text documentation, the business analyst does so in natural language, keeping the document as concise as possible.

Selecting the Appropriate Models

The requirements team describes what the organizational component that is undergoing change will look like in a series of graphical and text-format models. The straightforward approach below is adapted from David C. Hay's approach to requirements analysis, described in his book *Requirements Analysis: From Business Views to Architecture.*[3] Hays recommends creating the following component views of the enterprise:

+ **Data.** What information will be used by the solution?

+ **Business and function processes.** How will activities and business functions be handled in the solution?

+ **Organizations.** Who or what departments, groups, or business units will be involved in the project?

+ **Locations.** Where are these business groups located?

+ **Event-response-timing.** What events are in scope? What is the response to the event that must happen?

+ **Applications and technology.** What current information technology applications and infrastructure will be affected by the project?

+ **Business motivation.** Why are we investing in this project? What are the strategies and tactics, and the policies and business rules derived from them that constrain the business?

It must be noted that in some cases both current- and future-state models need to be built, whereas in others only one set of models is needed. See Table 6-3 to determine which models to build based on project type.

The following text describes the potential models that may be used to describe the organizational components listed above. Again, the intention of this book is not to describe the creation of each model in detail since there are many sources of information from which the reader can obtain that information. For step-by-step instructions for building most of the models mentioned here, refer to The *Software Requirements Memory Jogger* by Ellen Gottesdiener.[4]

Data Models

A *business data model* is a diagram that describes how data are represented in a business organization, an information system, or a database management system. At this point, the requirements team is interested only in creating data models that depict the information requirements of a business area, independent of the data design or a physical data storage mechanism. Alternative names for this model include *conceptual data model* and *logical data model*.

Table 6-3—Guide to Use of Current-State and Future-State Models

Type of Project	Current-State Models	Future-State Models
Business process reengineering project	X	X
Continuous process improvement project	X	X
Legacy system replacement project with no improvements	X	
Legacy system replacement project with significant business process redesign	X	X
New line of business project		X
Business transformation project	X	X

Because the data model is a picture of all the information necessary to run the business, it is often built using an *entity relationship diagram*, which is a standard modeling technique understood by many business analysts around the world. The business data model is owned by the business area experts. The business analyst typically captures the data requirements as described by the business experts during facilitated sessions. Additional complementary models might include the *class model*, which describes a collection of similar objects (i.e., persons, places, events, and physical artifacts) when using object-oriented development methods; *data tables*, used to validate a data model; and the *data dictionary*, an analysis model in the form of a repository of information describing the characteristics of the data structures and attributes needed by the system. Finally, each data entity should be defined in the *glossary*. See Figures 6-2 and 6-3 for sample data models.

Business Process and Function Models

Business process and function models get to the heart of the value stream of the business—what must be done to flow value through the business to the customer. We will discuss two process and function models, the *business process model* and the *use case model*.

Business Process Models

As discussed in the previous chapter, process models describe the current activities performed to operate the business and to meet the business goals and objectives. This step adds further detail to the process models likely to have been created during earlier scoping activities (discussed in Chapter 5), which depicted business processes in terms of the sequential steps and input and output flows across multiple functions, organizations, or job roles. Process models are used to help identify which steps in the process will be operated. The process models can be annotated to depict the use of manual or

Figure 6-2—Proton Data Sources

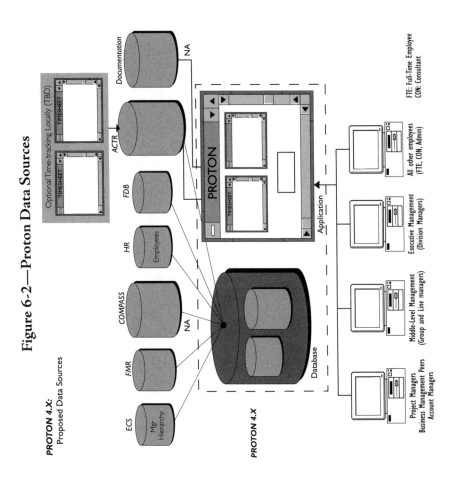

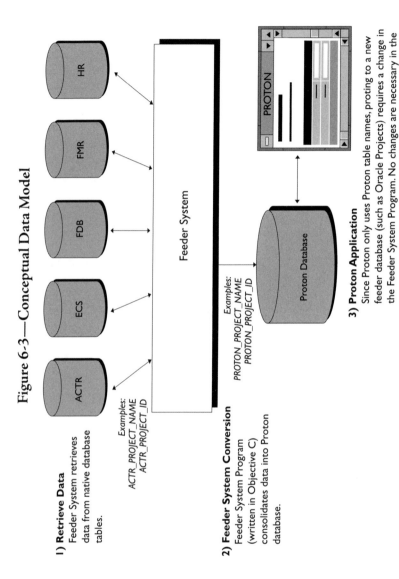

Figure 6-3—Conceptual Data Model

1) **Retrieve Data**
Feeder System retrieves data from native database tables.

Examples:
ACTR_PROJECT_NAME
ACTR_PROJECT_ID

2) **Feeder System Conversion**
Feeder System Program (written in Objective C) consolidates data into Proton database.

Examples:
PROTON_PROJECT_NAME
PROTON_PROJECT_ID

3) **Proton Application**
Since Proton only uses Proton table names, proting to a new feeder database (such as Oracle Projects) requires a change in the Feeder System Program. No changes are necessary in the base Proton application code or Proton database.

desktop tools, versus which steps will be allocated to a new software system. In essence, each major business process is identified, and a model is then created to represent the inherent activities associated with that process.

Along with data models, process models might be the diagramming technique used most often because they describe the actual cross-functional activities of the business. Process models are used extensively in business process improvement projects that might involve changes to non-IT process tools, such as workflows, job aids, policies, procedures, and other business documentation.

Additional complementary models may include *data flow diagrams*, which describe activities in terms of functions being performed, and *functional decomposition diagrams*, which are simple hierarchical representations of the functions performed by the business entity, starting with the organizational mission and then decomposed into several primary functions executed to achieve the mission And, finally, to relate data entities to functions, *function hierarchy models* are built to specify the data entities used by each function. The business process models are also owned by the business area experts. The business analyst typically captures the process and functional requirements as described by the business experts during facilitated sessions. See Figure 6-4 for a sample functional process map.

Use Case Models

Artifacts that elaborate on business process models include *use cases* and *user scenarios* or *stories*. These models describe the essential activities that must be supported by the new solution. The use-case approach describes the behavior of a system from the user's perspective. A use case identifies a sequence of actions performed by a system that yields an observable result of value or achieves a goal for the user. The use-case approach has many benefits:

+ Provides an early view of the intended functions

Figure 6-4—Financing Functional Process Map

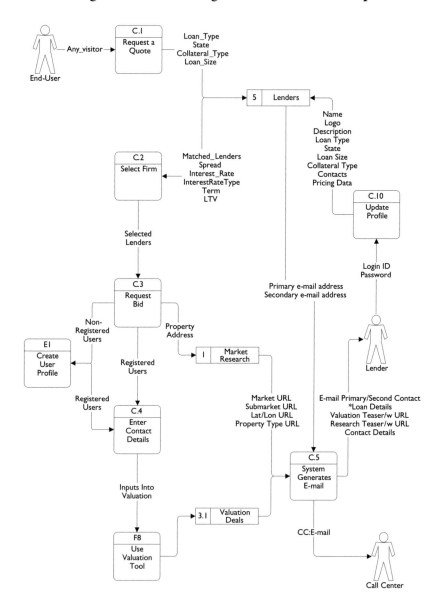

+ Provides the basis for producing the test case and end-user documentation

+ Provides insights into the intended behavior of the solution

+ Documents and tests alternative paths and exception conditions (which are the root cause of many defects not discovered until late in the development process or after implementation)

Use cases are written from the user's perspective. They describe how users will optimally use the system and how users might vary in their use of the system, referred to as alternative courses through the use case. A use case includes these standard elements:

+ A unique identification number

+ A header that provides high-level information about the use case, including name, brief description, and actors involved

+ A more detailed description that describes the use case goal

+ Pre- and post-conditions defining the requirements before and after the use case

+ A step-by-step elaboration of how the actor and system interact to accomplish the goal

+ Exceptions describing how to handle errors

+ Steps for variations for alternative paths through the use case

Figures 6-5 and 6-6 show examples of use cases.

Organization Models

Organization models define the existing organizational entities and the relationships between those entities. Organization models are most often represented in organization charts depicted in *hierar-*

Figure 6-5—Use Case Example

Use Case Status List

The following table lists the current status of each Use Case as of 1/08/07:

Use Case ID	Use Case Package	Use Case Name	Status
UC-1	General	User Logs In	Approved
UC-2	General	User Logs Out	Approved
UC-3	General	Guest Registers	Deferred

Actor List

The following two tables list the Actors that will interact with the DPD Portal:

Humans

Actor	Role	Priority
Policyholder/Insured Small Business Middle Market	External user/paying customer NOTE: For all Use Cases, Policyholder is at Company level and not Individual User level	1
Broker	External user/sales	1
Loss Control Staff	Internal user/access reports	3
Underwriter	Internal user/access reports	3
DPD Manager	Internal user/access reports/upload content/ track usage	2
System Administrator	Internal user/manage system	3
Customer Service Rep	Internal user/manage customers/track call volume	3
Guest	External user/prospect	4

Figure 6-5 (continued)

Systems

Actor	Role	Priority
Loss Control System	Loss Control Software	1
PQS	Policy Quote System	TBD
MPIS	Mainframe Policy Issue System	TBD
DMS	Document Management System	TBD
SAP	Billing System	TBD
Audit Submission Form	Audit submission	TBD
Loss Control News Feed(s)	Industry News/Bulletins	1

General Use Cases

UC-1: User Logs In

Goals

The USER LOGS IN USE CASE will meet one or more of the following User goals:

+ Enable the User to log into the DPD Portal.

A *User* in this context is any human who will directly access the DPD Portal, and can include any or all of the following Actors:

+ Policyholder
+ Broker
+ Loss Control Staff
+ Underwriter
+ DPD Manager
+ System Administrator
+ Customer Service Rep
+ Guest

Figure 6-5 (continued)

Use Case Status

This Use Case is currently APPROVED.

Preconditions

The User must already have a DPD Portal Username and Password [PORTAL ADDS NEW POLICYHOLDER/BROKER USE CASE].

State Drawing

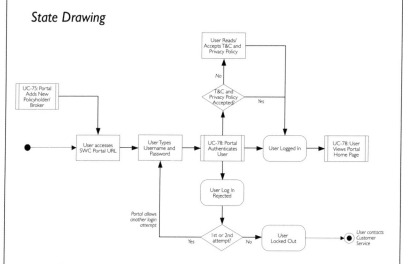

Main Process Flow

1. User opens browser software.

2. User accesses DPD Portal Website URL.

3. User types in Username and Password.

4. User clicks the Enter key.

5. DPD Portal verifies that User has entered valid ID and Password [PORTAL AUTHENTICATES USER USE CASE].

Figure 6-5 (continued)

Subflows

+ The User must read and accept DPD Portal Terms and Conditions and Privacy Policy before he/she can access the system.

+ If User enters an incorrect Username or Password, the DPD Portal will display an error message indicating this and asking the User to try again.

+ If the User does not successfully enter the correct Password within a pre-defined number of attempts (typically 3–5), the DPD Portal will lock access for that Username.

Alternate Flows

No Alternate Flows have been identified at this time.

Post Conditions

User will have access to the DPD Portal through the Portal Home Page [USER VIEWS PORTAL HOME PAGE USE CASE].

Open Issues

Date	Description / Resolution	Status
12/26/06	Need to discuss password incorrect lockout specification. Is there something documented on this?	Open
12/26/06	System will need to track User's acceptance of DPD Portal Terms and Conditions and Privacy Policy from first Log In	Open

Figure 6-5 (continued)

UC-2: User Logs Out

Goals

The USER LOGS OUT USE CASE will meet one or more of the following User goals:

- Enable the User to log into the DPD Portal.
- Help the User prevent unauthorized access to his/her account.

A User in this context is any human who will directly access the DPD Portal, and can include any or all of the following Actors:

- Policyholder
- Broker
- Loss Control Staff
- Underwriter
- DPD Manager
- System Administrator
- Customer Service Rep
- Guest

Use Case Status

This Use Case is currently APPROVED.

Preconditions

The User must be logged into the DPD Portal [USER LOGS IN USE CASE].

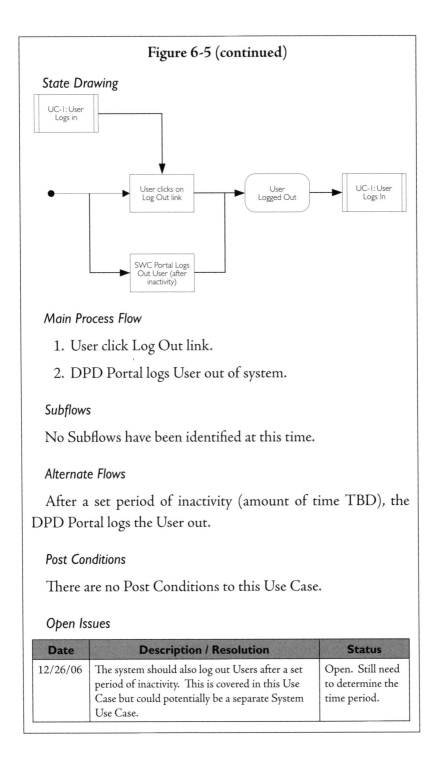

Figure 6-5 (continued)

State Drawing

Main Process Flow

1. User click Log Out link.

2. DPD Portal logs User out of system.

Subflows

No Subflows have been identified at this time.

Alternate Flows

After a set period of inactivity (amount of time TBD), the DPD Portal logs the User out.

Post Conditions

There are no Post Conditions to this Use Case.

Open Issues

Date	Description / Resolution	Status
12/26/06	The system should also log out Users after a set period of inactivity. This is covered in this Use Case but could potentially be a separate System Use Case.	Open. Still need to determine the time period.

Figure 6-5 (continued)

UC-3: Guest Registers

Goals

The GUEST REGISTERS USE CASE will meet one or more of the following User goals:

- Allow prospective DPD customers to access and view a limited subset of the DPD Portal.

- Show examples of the value-added services a prospect will obtain as a customer.

Use Case Status

This Use Case is Out-of-Scope for Phase 1 as of 1/05/07 and is DEFERRED.

Preconditions

There are no Preconditions to this Use Case.

State Drawing

Main Process Flow

1. Guest opens browser software.

2. Guest accesses DPD Portal Website URL.

3. Guest clicks Register link.

4. Guest completes Registration Form.

5. Guest reads/accepts DPD Portal Terms and Conditions; Privacy Policy.

6. DPD Portal verifies that Guest has entered valid Registration information and agreed to Terms and Conditions;

Figure 6-5 (continued)

Privacy Policy. [PORTAL AUTHENTICATES USER USE CASE].

Subflows

No Subflows have been identified at this time.

Alternate Flows

No Alternate Flows have been identified at this time.

Post Conditions

User will have access to the DPD Portal through the portal home page [USER VIEWS PORTAL HOME PAGE USE CASE].

Open Issues

Date	Description / Resolution	Status

Figure 6-6—Simple Use Case Model for a Customer to Get Cash from an ATM Machine

Use Case Name	Get Cash
Actors:	Customer, ATM machine
Description:	Customer requests cash from a selection of the accounts that he or she has active with the bank.
Preconditions:	1. Customer has an account at the bank. 2. Customer has a valid PIN.
Postconditions:	1. Customer account is reconciled or fails gracefully in case of system failure.
Normal course:	1. Customer selects fast cash, chooses an account, and selects withdrawal amount (a multiple of $20). 2. ATM notifies main banking system of customer account number and amount selected and receives acknowledgement plus the new balance. 3. ATM delivers the cash, card, and a receipt showing the new balance. 4. ATM logs the transaction.

chical decomposition diagrams, often accompanied by a description of the philosophy behind the organizational structure. Organizational structure dictates the reporting relationships, degree and type of horizontal and vertical interaction, methods for coordination and control, centralization versus decentralization of power, and the degree of formality of communications.

Organization models are supplemented by artifacts such as *stakeholder analysis matrix, roles and responsibilities tables, position descriptions*, and *competency models* for professions within the organization. In some cases, it might be necessary to create a model in the form of a matrix to depict information requirements by role.

Location Models

Location models describe where the business entity's operations are located. They often take the form of a *geographical map* pinpointing locations accompanied by a *matrix* describing the operational locations, the functions performed at each location, and the relationship among locations. Sometimes these models include information about the roles and responsibilities at each location and the communication that must take place between the various locations. Organizations strive to establish operational locations close to their customers that will best enable fulfillment of their mission and business objectives.

Event-Response Models

These models describe the role of an event (a stimulus that triggers a process to carry out a function), the response activated because of the event, and the role of time in the business operations. The model usually takes the form of an *event table* or *event list*. Examples of events are periodic planning cycles, receipt of an order, and hiring of a new employee. It is important to note that some business processes are strongly influenced by events and timing, whereas others are not.

Additional complementary models might include *state diagrams* and *state-data matrices*, analysis models that depict the life cycle of a data entity. See Figure 6-7 for a sample event-response model.

Application and Technology Models

Typically, the IT group has current views of the application systems and their interactions and the technical infrastructure supporting the enterprise. If the project will alter the application and technical infrastructure, the future views are created at a high level by the business analyst in collaboration with the technical lead. These models inform IT of the scope of technology change that will be needed because of the project. It is important to involve IT infrastructure representatives early in your project so that IT can plan for the changes that will be needed. See Figures 6-8 and 6-9 for examples.

Business Motivation Models

Business motivation models (BMM), developed by The Business Rules Group in 1995, are designed to capture the key concepts that drive business.[5] The BMM informs the organization about what motivates and what constrains the enterprise. The model includes the following information about the business:

- Vision and mission

- Goals, objectives, strategies, and tactics to achieve the vision and mission

- Business policies and *business rules* list mapped to the *data models* and *function models*

We have now discussed two of the three primary activities in the requirements analysis and specification processes—analyzing scope

Figure 6-7—Event-Response Model to Initiate a Project

Tracking #	Description	Priority
EV-PR-0001	Project starts • User accesses Create Project page • System generates and displays a Project ID • System populates Project Name field with the Project ID • User either overwrites the Project Name with a different name or retains the Project ID as the name	1
EV-PR-0002	Data is entered into project • User selects or enters general project information (such as description, budget amount, etc.) • User selects links, categories/keywords, attachments, and/or security attributes to add to project	1
EV-PR-0003	Project is saved • User selects the save function • System posts and updates data on the central project database	1
EV-PR-0004	Project is linked to notebook, project, submission, sample, or result • User creates links to notebook, project, submission, sample, or result (described in *Data is entered into project* above) • Clicking on a hyperlink will open the selected object to permit viewing and editing of the linked object	2
EV-PR-0005	Project is modified • User selects existing project from navigation screen/menu • User selects and changes general project information (such as name, description, budget amount, etc.) • User adds or edits categories/keywords, links, attachments and/or security attributes to the project	2
EV-PR-0006	Project is deleted • User selects existing active project • User uses delete function • Project retains project and project history • Project removes project from system	2
EV-PR-0007	Project is canceled • User selects existing active project • User enters reason for cancel • User executes cancel function • Project updates project status • Project removes project from general user access	3

Figure 6-8—Development Projects in Proton

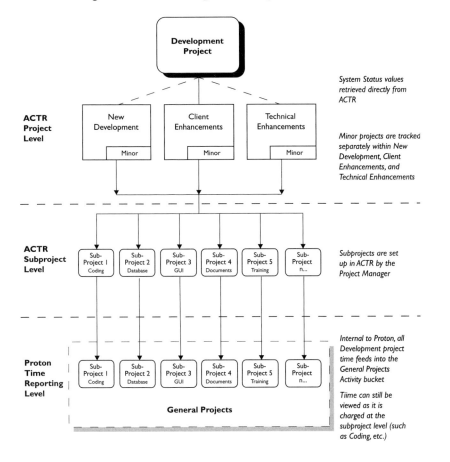

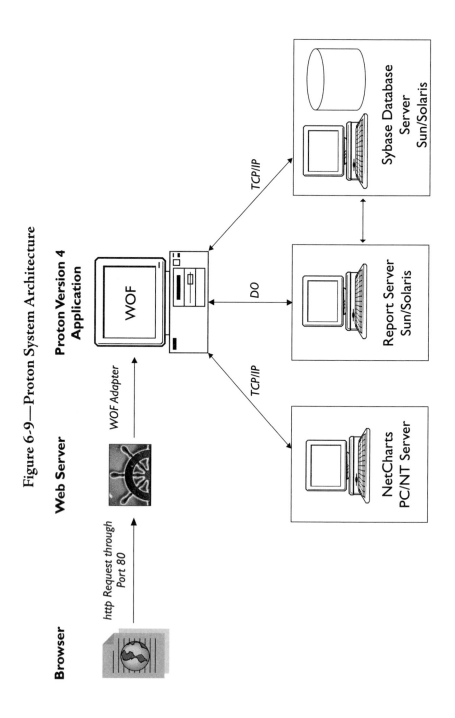

Figure 6-9—Proton System Architecture

and analyzing requirements. The next chapter discusses the third stage, specifying requirements for the new business solution.

Endnotes

1. Scott Ambler. *Agile Models Distilled: Potential Artifacts for Agile Modeling*. Online at http://www.agilemodeling.com/artifacts (accessed July 26, 2006). Table 6-1 adapted with permission.

2. Scott Ambler. *Agile/Lean Documentation: Strategies for Agile Software Development*. Online at http://www.agilemodeling.com/essays/agileDocumentation.htm (accessed July 26, 2006). Table 6-2 adapted with permission.

3. David C. Hay. *Requirements Analysis: From Business Views to Architecture*, 2003. Upper Saddle River, NJ: Prentice Hall PTR.

4. Ellen Gottesdiener. *The Software Requirements Memory Jogger*, 2006. Salem, NH: OAL/QPC.

5. The Business Rules Group. *The Business Motivation Model: Business Governance in a Volatile World*. Online at http://www.businessrulesgroup.org/second_paper/BRG-BMM.pdf (accessed August 9, 2007).

Chapter 7

Specifying Requirements

In This Chapter:

- Requirements Specification in Practice
- Categorizing Requirements
- Deriving Requirements
- Assigning Requirements Attributes
- Prioritizing Requirements
- Validating Requirements

Specification activities involve *translating* the collective requirements into written requirements specifications that are in terms that can be understood by all stakeholders. This task typically involves substantial time and effort, because each stakeholder might have different expertise, perspectives, and expectations of the requirements. *Requirement specifications* are elaborated from and linked to the scoping and analysis models and structured into a logical framework providing a *repository of requirements*. It is through this progressive elaboration that the requirements team often detects areas that are not defined in sufficient detail, which unless addressed can lead to uncontrolled change to system requirements.

The Software Engineering Institute defines a requirements specification as a document that prescribes, in a complete, precise, verifiable manner, the requirements, design, behavior, or characteristics of a system or system component.[1] The specification of what is to be accomplished integrates all of the requirement artifacts that have been created. Specification takes the complete set of requirements models and organizes them into a cohesive, structured whole so that they can be easily used and understood by the development team. Specification, in essence, is the process of organizing, refining, and finalizing the requirements. The final deliverable from the specification process is the requirements specification document, which includes or references the entire collection of requirements artifacts that together comprise the business requirements. If you are using a requirements management software tool, the final deliverable from the specification process is a database of requirements artifacts.

During the specifying process, the business analyst continues to work collaboratively with the customers and end-users of the new solution and key members of the solution development team. Typically, the business analyst completes the *business requirements document (BRD)*, which includes or references all artifacts that have been created during requirements elicitation and analysis. In some cases, more than one text deliverable might result from the specifying process. Other types of and names for requirements specification documents include the *requirements document, business requirements document, use case document, concept of operations (ConOps), requirements definition, requirements statement, system definition, functional specification, supplemental specification,* and *technical specification.* Minimally, a business requirements document is created. (See Appendix D for an example of a business requirements document template.)

While it appears that specifying requirements is one of the last activities in the requirements definition process, the business analyst has likely been drafting and refining the requirements document(s) throughout the process. The final specification activities take place after the business analyst has analyzed scope (covered in Chapter 5) and requirements (covered in Chapter 6). However, in addition to organizing the business requirements documentation, requirements specification involves progressively elaborating and refining the requirements. This final specification step reveals omissions, prevents loss of requirements, and provides a means to communicate with stakeholders. Therefore, the specification activities inevitably take you back to refine the analysis artifacts created during previous steps in the process. During this activity, as requirements are finalized, they are continuously validated by both the business and technical teams. The value of creating a requirements specification document is that it:

+ Provides an overarching document that integrates all requirements artifacts

+ Provides detail, in text form, for information not represented in the scoping and analysis models

+ Drives consensus among various stakeholder groups on what the new system must do

+ Serves as a vehicle to obtain agreement on the part of the business and technical teams that the business need is understood

+ Serves as a bridge between business and system requirements[2]

Regardless of the number of documents produced for the deliverable of the specification process, the components of the specification document remain the same. Referencing Hay once more,[3] a typical requirements specification document contains the following information that was gathered during preproject business analysis, requirements elicitation, and analysis activities:

+ The purpose of the document

+ Related documents

+ The project purpose

- The sources for the end user requirements

- The required business capabilities and functions, including:

  - Missing data and functions

  - Use cases or feature-based requirement components to describe how the system will work

- System constraints

- Supplemental (nonfunctional) requirements

  - Quality requirements

  - Response-time requirements

  - Look and feel requirements

  - Security requirements

  - Cultural and political requirements

  - Legal requirements

- Proposed level of technology

- Capacity requirements

- Make or buy decision

- Stakeholder criteria for success

  - Performance characteristics

  - Context of implementation

  - Stakeholder constraints

  - Measures of success

□ Requirements validation criteria

+ Appendices, which may include a glossary, data dictionary, the context diagram, use cases and scenarios, and reference to any additional requirements information

Requirements Specification in Practice

In addition to drafting the requirements specification document, the important specification activities, described in detail in the rest of the chapter, are categorizing, deriving, assigning attributes, and prioritizing requirements.

Categorizing Requirements

Requirements are categorized into types depending on their source and applicability. Understanding requirements types helps in documenting and prioritizing requirements. It also enables the technical team to conduct trade-off analysis, estimate the system cost and schedule, and better assess the level of changes to be expected. Finally, reviewing the list of requirements types can aid the business analyst in identifying areas that might require further investigation. Typically, requirements are broadly characterized as *functional* or *supplemental* (a.k.a. *nonfunctional*). In addition, *constraints* imposed upon the requirements and/or the solution are captured as part of the categorizing process.

Functional Requirements

Functional requirements describe capabilities the system will have in terms of behaviors or operations triggering a specific system action or response. Functional requirements are best expressed as a verb or verb phrase. Functional requirements are written so as not to unnecessarily constrain the solution, thus providing a firm foundation for the system architects. Functional requirements include:

+ Specifications of the system functionality (what the system or product does). For example: "The system shall allow a scheduler to assign a staff person to a particular shift."

+ Actions the system must take (check, calculate, record, retrieve). For example: "When no staff person is available for a particular shift, the system shall allow the scheduler to select an individual from a list of contractors."

Functional specifications are often defined by use cases, which are an effective way to organize functional requirements. Each use case constitutes a complete course of action initiated by an actor, and it specifies the interaction that takes place between the actor and the system. The collected use cases specify all the existing ways of using the system. Several sources providing excellent information about the use case approach are available because the approach is gaining in popularity due to its straightforward methodology. Two that we suggest are:

+ *Use Cases, Requirements in Context* by Daryl Kulak and Eamonn Guiney, published by Addison Wesley. This text suggests a use-case-driven approach using four iterations to complete the use case documents.

+ *The Software Requirements Memory Jogger* by Ellen Gottesdiener, published by GOAL/QPC. This book provides a step-by-step process to build a use case, accompanied by tips and examples.

Supplemental Requirements

Supplemental requirements, also known as *nonfunctional requirements,* stipulate a physical or performance characteristic and serve as constraints on system capabilities. *Supplemental requirements* are properties or qualities that make the solution attractive, usable, fast, or reliable, and they are typically captured in a section of the *business requirements document* or in a stand-alone *supplemental requirements document*. Examples include:

+ *Look and feel requirements*—the appearance of the user interfaces and reports

+ *Usability requirements*—the ease of use, and any special usability considerations

+ *Performance requirements*—how fast, how safe, and how accurate the functionality must be

+ *Operational requirements*—the operating environment of the system, and what considerations must be made for this environment

+ *Maintainability and portability requirements*—expected changes, and the time allowed to make them

+ *Security requirements*—the security and confidentiality of the information contained within the system

+ *Cultural and political requirements*—special requirements that come about because of the people involved in the product's development and operations

Constraints

Constraints pose restrictions on the acceptable solution options. *Technical constraints* might include the requirement to use a predetermined language or database, or specific hardware. Technical constraints might also specify restrictions such as message size and timing, software size, maximum number of and size of files, records, data elements, and any enterprise architecture standards to which the system must adhere. *Business constraints* include budget limitations, restrictions on the people who can do the work, and skill sets available.

Technical and business constraints pose restrictions on the design of a system or the process by which a system is developed. They do not affect the external behavior of the system, but they must be fulfilled to meet technical, business, or contractual obligations. While the sources are varied, design constraints typically originate from one of three sources:

- Restriction of design options (e.g., use a specific DBMS)

- Conditions imposed on the development process (often based on existing infrastructure and the business environment)

- Regulations and imposed standards

During the project initiation process, business constraints are identified and documented. The business analyst validates them and continues to uncover additional constraints throughout the elicitation, analysis, and specification process. Likewise, the business analyst collaborates with the technical team to identify a complete set of technical constraints.

Deriving Requirements

Many requirements that have been captured need to be further developed, or *derived*, to add detail, remove ambiguity, and increase clarity. Four commonly used techniques—parsing, interpreting, focusing, and qualifying—help the business analyst in deriving requirements.

Parsing Requirements

The business analyst uses this technique to decompose requirements that are too broad to be implemented without error. Such requirements statements need to be broken down into more detailed statements. This decomposition separates a single requirements statement into multiple requirements. It is a one-to-many relationship. An example of this technique follows.

Source requirement:

+ "User-completed fields on tax forms shall be converted to electronic text documents."

The parsed requirements would be:

+ "The system shall be able to convert handwriting to text."

+ "The system shall be able to convert machine print to text."

+ "The system shall be able to electronically correct user-completed fields."

Another example of parsing would be to take a compound requirement and separate it. Although the use of "and" is grammatically and logically correct where multiple things have to be accomplished, it has no place in stating requirements. The risk is too high that only one condition will be tested and the others overlooked. For traceability, it is important for the parsed requirement to reference the original requirement. The original requirement should also reference all parsed requirements.

Interpreting Requirements

Stakeholders might state requirements that are very general in nature but are, nonetheless, true needs. Business analysts must be able to interpret the requirements and create new requirements that can then be validated. The new requirements are generated to reduce ambiguity. This requires that the business analyst work closely with the customer/end-user. An example follows:

Source requirement:

+ "Each PC shall have state-of-the-art software installed."

Interpreted requirement:

+ "Each PC shall have MS 2003 Professional running under Windows XP Professional installed."

This is usually a one-to-one relationship. It involves ensuring that the new requirement references the original and that it maintains the same category as the original. It is also important that the original requirement trace forward to the newly created interpreted requirement.

Focusing Requirements

The process of focusing requirements involves examining all the requirements within their categories. As requirements are collected from all the various sources and are categorized, there is a high probability that there will be duplication among the requirements. Duplicated requirements are also referred to as *overlapping requirements*. The process of focusing takes the overlapping requirements and combines them into one very focused and clear requirement. An example would be:

Source requirement:

+ "Each PC must have a standard spreadsheet tool installed that runs under Windows."

Focused requirement:

+ "Each PC on the LAN shall have Microsoft Office Excel 2003 installed."

Qualifying Requirements

Business analysts must sometimes generate requirements because stakeholder requirements are often incomplete or ambiguous. Qualification requirements are added to the requirements list to provide a method of verification or compliance. This is usually a one-to-many relationship. An example follows:

Source requirement:

+ "The xxx command must perform the following actions . . ."

Qualified requirement:

+ "Each command shall be executed during system testing to demonstrate its functionality."

In this example, the customer provided a list of actions that a given command must perform with little detail of what each action does. The business analyst has added that each command will be demonstrated during system testing. Once again, the original requirement now references the qualified requirement for traceability. Also important is that the qualified requirement, properly documented, now points to the original requirement.

Assigning Requirements Attributes

Specification activities also involve identifying all the precise attributes of each unique requirement. This process helps gain an understanding of the relative importance of each requirement. Attributes are used for a variety of purposes to manage and use requirements, including explanation, selection, filter, and validation. In addition, attributes enable the association of data with objects, table markers, table cells, modules, and projects.[4] Attributes may be user-defined or system-defined. They allow the requirements team to associate information with individual or related groups of requirements, and they often facilitate the requirements analysis process by filtering and sorting. Typical attributes attached to requirements might include:

+ *Unique identifier* that does not change. The reference is not to be reused if the requirement is moved, changed, or deleted. This identifier can be alpha, numeric, or some combination of alpha and numeric. This identifier stays with the requirement from its original capture through its life in the project.

- *Acceptance criteria* describe the nature of the test that would demonstrate to customers, end-users, and stakeholders that the requirement has been met. Acceptance criteria are usually captured from the end users by asking the question, "What kind of assessment would satisfy you that this requirement has been met?"

- *Author* of the requirement refers to who wrote it.

- *Complexity* indicates how difficult the requirement will be to implement.

- *Ownership* specifies the individual or group that needs the requirement. The owner of the original requirement and the owner's authority to state requirements should be documented.

- *Performance* addresses how the requirement must be met.

- *Stability* is used to indicate how mature the requirement is. This attribute is used to determine whether the requirement is firm enough to begin work on it.

- *Urgency* refers to how soon the requirement is needed.

- *Business value*, or the rationale for including the requirement, helps prioritize features in terms of business value.

- *Status* of the requirement denotes whether it is proposed, accepted, verified with the users, or implemented.

- *Type* of requirement identifies whether the requirement is functional, nonfunctional, or a constraint. Requirement types are discussed in further detail later in this chapter.

- *Priority* of the requirement rates its relative importance at a given point in time. Prioritization is discussed in further detail later in this chapter.

- *Source* of the requirement identifies who requested it. Every requirement should originate from a source that has the authority to specify requirements. This might or might not be the same as the requirement owner. Requirement sources are discussed in further detail below.

When attributing the requirement to a *source*, whether it came from a *hard source* or a *soft source*, the source should be noted. Hard-source requirements usually indicate the following:

+ What needs to be delivered

+ When it needs to be delivered

+ Who the client/customer/recipient is

+ What the applicable standards are

+ What the obligations and commitments are

The hard-source requirements are typically generated by others and represent some form of agreement. They are already in place and were created prior to the start or outside the boundaries of a given project. This information may come from a variety of sources across the stakeholder group. Examples of hard sources of requirements include:

+ Requests for proposal (RFP)

+ Statements of work (SOW)

+ Contracts

+ Specifications

- Standards (industry, government, client)

- Reference documents (user guides, manuals)

- Customer meetings (minutes, session notes)

- Project plans

- Systems engineering documentation

- Operations procedures and manuals

Soft-source requirements reveal how things really work. Gathering requirements from soft sources involves a greater amount of interaction with the client than do hard-source requirements. Soft-source requirements are captured in the documents created as a result of requirements elicitation and analysis. The *modeling techniques* outlined in the previous chapters would certainly qualify as *soft-source requirements*. Some examples of soft sources of requirements are:

- Surveys and questionnaires

- Interviews

- Customer workshops

- Simulations

- Usability studies

- Prototypes and models

Prioritizing Requirements

A common problem is that there are too many functions and features to implement within business time and cost constraints. The requirements need to be prioritized according to business value and other important considerations. Decisions about priorities are complex because they involve many different factors that could be in conflict with each other. Stakeholders often have different and conflicting goals, often leading to difficulty reaching agreement about priorities.

Prioritization Factors

Some of the factors that affect the prioritization of requirements are listed below.[5] Not all of these factors are relevant to every project. The importance of the factors could change from project to project. Additionally, not all factors are equally important to all stakeholders.

- Value to the business (how much the business will benefit)

- Value to customer (how much this will increase customer satisfaction)

- Minimize cost of implementation (how much cost to develop)

- Time to implement (how much time to deliver)

- Ease of technical implementation (how technically difficult)

- Ease of business implementation (how organizationally difficult)

- Obligation to some external authority (law, regulation, contract)

Prioritization Techniques

A method often used to begin the process of prioritization is to determine customer satisfaction/dissatisfaction as it relates to each requirement. This is a good technique to help various stakeholders make difficult prioritization choices and to predict customer satisfaction. Instead of using a low, medium, or high priority scale, two questions are asked:

+ On a scale of 1–5, how satisfied will you be if we implement this requirement?

+ On a scale of 1–5, how dissatisfied will you be if we do not implement this requirement?

This approach gets the stakeholders away from a simple binary decision or a simple high, medium, or low decision.

Another technique to prioritize requirements is to use a grid that refers to importance and urgency. Every requirement can be considered urgent or not urgent, and important or not important. High-priority requirements are both important (the stakeholder needs the capability) and urgent (the stakeholder needs it in the next release). Contractual or legal obligations might dictate that the requirement must be included, or there might be compelling business reasons to implement it promptly. Medium-priority requirements are important (the stakeholder needs the capability) but not urgent (they can wait for later releases). Low-priority requirements are not important (the stakeholder can live without the capability if necessary) and not urgent (the stakeholder can wait, perhaps forever). The last category is urgent but not really important. Do not waste time on these requirements because they do not add sufficient value to the business.

Another approach might be to use the terms *critical, important,* and *useful. Critical* means indispensable, suggesting that a stakeholder would not be able to use a solution without this feature. Without this feature, the system would not fulfill its primary mission or meet the business need. *Important* means that without the feature there would be a significant loss of customer utility, perhaps even market share or revenue, or new customer segments served. If the important items were not implemented, some users would like the product and others would not buy/use it. *Useful* means that the feature would be nice to have but is not critical or important.

It is a challenge to keep the prioritization process as simple as possible but rigorous enough to ensure that you are prioritizing *predominantly on business value.* Strive to move requirements away from the political arena to a forum in which stakeholders can make honest assessments. Doing so will give the project a better probability of building the solution that will deliver the maximum business value. As organizations mature in the management of critical projects, requirements are bundled into releases, and each release is prioritized based on business value. It is the business analyst who continually emphasizes the need to prioritize requirements based on business value.

Validating Requirements

The business analyst continually works to ensure the integrity of the written requirements statements. As mentioned, precise text requirements statements transform analysis models into understandable written statements, provide the business rationale for the initiative, and provide clarity for the solution design. All the requirements information that has been captured through the elicitation, analysis, and specification is now scrutinized in order for it to be considered a set of "good" requirements. The usefulness and accuracy of the requirements effort depend on how well the requirements statements are written. There is little benefit to developing a thorough understanding of the problem if that understanding is not effectively communicated to customers, designers, implementers, maintainers, and testers. When validating requirements, look for these basic documentation principles:

+ Requirements must be realistic.

+ Functionality must be defined.

+ Behavior must be represented.

Characteristics of Good Requirements

The following are characteristics of good requirements. During validation activities, check for these characteristics.

- **Allocatable.** The requirement can be allocated to a component of the system design, where it can be implemented.

- **Attainable.** The requirement is technically feasible and fits within the project funding and time constraints.

- **Complete.** All known requirements are documented, and all conditions under which a requirement applies are stated.

- **Concise.** The shorter the specification the better.

- **Consistent.** The requirements can be met without causing conflict with any of the other requirements.

- **Correct.** Every requirement stated represents something required of the system or product to be built. Each requirement must accurately describe the functionality to be built. Only the customer, user, or stakeholder who was the source of the requirement can determine its *correctness*.

- **Design-independent.** The specification does not imply a specific architecture. Requirements are stated in a way that allows all possible designs. This characteristic is also referred to as *solution-independent*.

- **Feasible.** It is possible to implement each requirement within the capabilities and limitations of the business, technical, and operational environment.

- **Measurable and testable.** The requirement can be tested to ensure that it meets measures of success. This characteristic is also referred to as *verifiable*. The requirement states something that can be confirmed by examination, analysis, test, or demonstration. A good requirement does not contain words that are not *testable* and *measurable*. If it is impossible to ensure that the requirement is met in the system, the requirement should be removed or revised. The verification method and level at which the requirement can be verified (i.e., the location in the system where the requirement is met) should be determined explicitly as part of the development of each requirement. Requirements statements that include words that have relative meaning are not verifiable.

+ **Modifiable.** A specification's structure and style should be developed in such a way that any necessary changes can be made easily, completely, and consistently.

+ **Necessary.** The requirement is essential to meet the business goals and objectives. If the system can meet prioritized, real needs without it, the requirement is not necessary. The requirement should be traceable to a goal stated in the project charter, vision document, business case, or other initiating document.

+ **Organized.** Requirements contained within the specification are easy to locate.

+ **Prioritized.** Prioritize requirements to determine which are essential, desirable, or optional. A *priority* is assigned to each functional requirement or feature to indicate how essential it is to a particular system release. The most important factor when prioritizing is business value.

+ **Traceable.** The origin (source) of the requirement must be known and the requirement can be referenced or located throughout the system. (Note: an automated requirements traceability tool enables finding the location in the system where each requirement is met.) *Traceable backwards:* Each requirement should be traced back to specific customer, user, or stakeholder input, such as a use case, a business rule, or some other origin. *Traceable forward*: Each requirement should have a unique identifier that assists in identifying the requirement, maintaining its change history, and tracing the requirement through the system components.

+ **Unambiguous.** Every requirement stated has only one interpretation. All readers of a requirement should arrive at the same interpretation of its meaning. Requirements written in simple, concise, straightforward language are more likely to be unambiguous. All specialized terms and terms that might be subject to confusion should be well defined.

+ **Understandable.** Both business and technical stakeholders comprehend and approve the requirements for use. *Understandable* means that the requirements must be clear, concise, simple, and free from ambiguity. Ambiguous requirements are often misunderstood, resulting in rework and corrective actions during the design, development, and testing phases. If the requirement can be interpreted in more than one way, it should be removed or clarified. When writing requirements, the author should use simple, short sentences and imperative phrases using *shall*. Statements indicating *goals* or using the word *will* are not imperatives.

Guidelines for Producing Valid Requirements

To achieve these characteristics, there is a set of guidelines. Following these guidelines will help ensure that your requirements are valid.

+ Requirements statements use the word *shall*. This is a keyword used to differentiate requirements statements.

+ There should be only one *shall* for each uniquely identified requirements statement.

- Requirements should be written in short, simple sentences.

- Terminology should be used consistently throughout.

- Requirements should be stated positively.

- Requirements should be grammatically correct.

- Requirements should be accompanied by sufficient notes and comments to support them.

- Requirements should be written in the imperative. Requirements are a statement of work to be performed; even though a requirement is included in a contract, using non-imperative words makes implementation of the requirement optional.

- Do not use the words *will* and *should* in stating requirements. *Will* is used in statements of fact, and *should* is used in goals. In addition, troubled words should be resolved. The following are examples of such words along with their translations:

  □ Or—Select one of the options.

  □ Can, should, may, might—Express a desire rather than a requirement; may choose not to implement.

  □ Must—Assign 100 percent reliability.

  □ Are, is, will—Use in descriptive section or as a lead-in to a requirement.

  □ Support, and/or—Confusing and often costly.

  □ But not limited to, etc.—Incomplete thought

- *Shall* means "prescribes" and is used to dictate the specification of a functional capability.

- *Will* means "describes" and is used to cite things that the operational environment is to provide to the capability being specified.

- *Must* and *must not* imply constraints. *Must* is often used to establish performance requirements constraints.

- *Should* means "suggest" and is not used as an imperative in writing requirements statements.

- Finally, for good requirements avoid the use of:

  - Adequate

  - Approximately

  - Better than

  - Comparison

  - Easy

  - Maintainable

  - Maximize

  - Minimize

  - Normally

  - Optimize

  - Quality product

  - Quick

  - Rapid

  - Substantial

- □ Sufficient to

- □ Timely

Endnotes

1. The Software Engineering Institute. *SEI Open Systems Glossary*. Online at http://www.sei.cmu.edu/opensystems/glossary.html#s (accessed August 13, 2007). SEI references the International Institute of Electrical and Electronic Engineers. *Draft Guide for Information Technology—Portable Operating System Interface*, 1993. New York, NY: Portable Applications Standard Committee of the IEEE Computer Society.

2. Ellen Gottesdiener. *The Software Requirements Memory Jogger*, 2006. Salem, NH: OAL/QPC.

3. David C. Hay. *Requirements Analysis: From Business Views to Architecture*, 2003. Upper Saddle River, NJ: Prentice Hall PTR.

4. Richard Stevens, Peter Brook, Ken Jackson, and Stuart Arnold. *Systems Engineering, Coping with Complexity*, 1998. Upper Saddle River, NJ: Pearson, Prentice Hall.

5. Volere Requirements Resources. The Atlantic Systems Guild, Inc. *Prioritization Analysis*. Online at http://www.volere.co.uk/pa1.htm (accessed August 14, 2007).

Part III
Other Considerations

ow that the requirements are specified and the full set of documentation exists, the requirements must be approved by key stakeholders. In addition, the requirements documentation must be baselined and put under change control. As the solution is developed, the requirements must be traced through the solution design, construction, and test activities to ensure all critical and important requirements are satisfied. These processes are the topic of Chapter 8. Chapter 9 provides an insight into analysis best practices that are emerging within the business analysis industry. And Chapter 10 closes out our discussion by providing a view from an expert practitioner on how to choose the right requirements analysis techniques for your project.

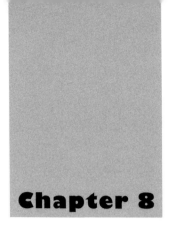

Chapter 8

Requirements Management

In This Chapter:

- Securing Requirements Approval

- Baselining Requirements

- Managing Changes to Requirements

- Tracing Requirements through the BSLC

At this point, the requirements have been analyzed, specified, organized, validated, and stored in a repository. The next step is to secure approval from all key stakeholders.

Securing Requirements Approval

The final activities that mark the end of the requirements phase are a series of requirements reviews and approval by the business team, the technical team, and the project sponsor.

Review and Approval of the Business Team

The business analyst facilitates final reviews with the business team to ensure that the requirements are complete and accurate. To accomplish this, the business analyst conducts one or more working sessions with the business SMEs to secure approval from the business standpoint. Even though the business analyst has been working with the business SMEs throughout the process, some minor enhancements and improvements to the requirements will likely be identified during these reviews. The business analyst updates the requirements artifacts as appropriate and then conducts similar sessions with the technical SMEs.

Review and Approval of the Technical Team

During the requirements analysis and specification process, the technical lead and other technical SMEs have been working closely with the business analyst as key members of the requirements team. As requirements models and specifications emerge, the technical lead (also referred to as the solution architect) begins to create the high-level design of the solution. The technical lead facilitates discussion among the core team and other technical SMEs to identify potential solutions and conduct trade-off analysis of the solution options to determine the best solution in terms of cost, schedule, risk, and quality. In addition, the make/buy decision is made collaboratively by members the core project team. These early solution-design activities are iterative, and they take place concurrent with the requirements specification activities because solution design constraints can affect requirements. Remember that valid requirements must be *technically feasible*. So, as the solution design changes, the requirements might change to accommodate the design constraints, as well as the cost and schedule constraints.

After the business team approves the requirements, the business analyst facilitates final reviews with the technical team to ensure that the requirements are mature enough and are structured adequately for design and development to begin in earnest. To accomplish this, the business analyst conducts one or more working sessions with the technical SMEs to secure approval from a solution development standpoint.

Review and Approval of the Project Sponsor and/or Governance Group

A major control gate for projects occurs upon completing the requirements. At this *control gate review* (also referred to as a *phase gate review* or a *stage gate review*), the business analyst, project manager, and business and technical leads present the requirements, the high-level solution design, and the make/buy decision to management for formal approval. Ideally, the project sponsor first approves the approach, followed by a review and approval by members of the portfolio management governance group. The lower-level reviews with business and technical stakeholders have already taken place, and the requirements have been approved by them.

During the requirements development process, much is learned about the project. Prior to the control gate review, the project manager reviews and updates key project documentation as appropriate. It is almost certain that the project baseline plans, including the schedule, cost, scope, and risk estimates will now need to be updated. It is also possible that the business case has changed. So this control gate review is not only about approving the requirements and solution concept, but it is also about providing management with the salient information needed to determine whether continued investment in the project is warranted.

To develop new cost, time, and risk estimates, the project manager collaborates with the business analyst and the technical and business SMEs to create updated plans for the design, construction, and test phases. In addition, plans for the transition to establish the new business solution as a component of the enterprise are established at a high level so management can begin to understand the scope of change that will take place within the business. Transition activities include restructuring within the impacted business and/or technical units; education and training of business and technical staff and/or acquiring additional staff; development of new policies, procedures, and job aids; purchase and implementation of new desktop tools;

implementation of software and hardware; and conversion of data. Finally, the cost of operating the system in the business and technical environments is included in the estimates.

Upon securing approval to proceed with design and construction (or to purchase and integrate a COTS solution), the business analyst baselines the requirements, implements a formal requirements change control process, and transitions into requirements management activities in support of solution design efforts.

Baselining Requirements

Baselining the requirements occurs immediately after the formal review and approval process mentioned above. The business requirements document(s) and accompanying models have been reviewed and approved by key stakeholders. The complete set of requirements and any supporting documentation form the *requirements baseline*, which is the base upon which change requests will be evaluated for design, development, cost, and schedule implications.

The baselining process may be as simple as putting version control on all the requirements artifacts. These would include the business documents, as well as solution designs and any software/hardware requirements that might have been developed by systems analysts concurrently. Publishing the baseline for the project team affords everyone access to and knowledge of the versions in effect. This simple step gives the team the ability to distinguish between outdated and current requirements. This set of requirements includes those that have been added, changed, or deleted throughout the review and approval activities. It is important to note that a deleted requirement still remains in the documentation archives but is labeled "deleted."

Managing Changes to Requirements

To understate the obvious, requirements engineering is a difficult and risky business. Ideally, we would like to get a clear and thorough picture of the requirements before development, obtain customer sign-off on these requirements, and then set up procedures that manage requirements changes. Regardless of the care taken, however, requirements will change because:

+ The business environment is dynamic. In today's economy, fundamental business forces are rapidly changing the value of system features. What may be a good set of requirements now may not be so in a few months or a year.

+ Everything in business systems development depends on the requirements. The assumption that fixed requirements are not the norm also means the baseline plan is subject to change.

+ Estimation is difficult for business solutions with significant IT components because they are basically research and development endeavors. The nature of IT systems is intangible, and the real value is difficult to predict.

Because changes to the requirements baseline are inevitable, we need a process that is efficient and effective for managing change. The change management process puts the team in control so that it can discover changes early, perform impact analysis, and incorporate the changes that are deemed necessary and acceptable into the solution in a systematic manner. The goals are to *welcome change that adds value to the business* and to *reduce the cost of change* through incremental development. Change management can be established by implementing procedures for the four simple steps listed below. These activities can be performed by a member of the project team who owns the change control process or by the core team working collaboratively:

+ Document and evaluate the change justification.

+ Assess the impact of the change.

+ Accept, reject, or defer the change.

+ Implement the change if approved.

Step 1: Document and Evaluate the Change Justification

Documenting the change involves a formal but simple process. This process includes a standard change request form and a change log. Pertinent and predetermined information is captured on the change request form. The request is then captured in the change log. The process ensures that the key information is present, including the change's justification and rationale, the owner, and the source.

Step 2: Assess the Impact of the Change

First, the change request is examined to see if it is in alignment with the mission/vision of the project. If this initial screening is passed, the impact of the change is assessed. Performing a change impact assessment requires determining (1) the impact of the requested change on the business solution and (2) the impact of the requested change on the project cost, time, scope, and risk. The impact on the project is important, but it can be determined only after an analysis of the full impact on the solution under development. In addition, a decision is made as to where the change will be implemented. The change might impact the actual user requirements, functional requirements, architecture or design artifacts, software code, hardware configuration, interfaces, and test plans.

Step 3: Accept, Reject, or Defer the Change

Finally, when the full range of potential change impacts has been assessed, it is appropriate to look at the effect the change will have on the business value of the solution and the budget, schedule, risk, and resources. The decision to accept, reject, or defer a change request is usually the domain of a change control board (CCB). CCBs are typically established for significant projects—those that are large, highly complex, and high-risk.

For the CCB to be effective, its responsibilities should be defined, documented, and agreed to by key stakeholders. Most CCBs live outside the project at the program or portfolio level. The group convenes regularly to evaluate and make decisions regarding all pending change requests and to review the status of the project. As changes are approved, it is likely that requirement priorities will change. This might affect how and when various requirements are implemented. Once the CCB has approved a change, the CCB will often reprioritize requirements.

Step 4: Implement the Change if Approved

The timing for implementing the change should be well thought out and planned into the overall schedule. Many organizations use another technique/form known as *authorization to proceed*, which formally informs interested parties that it is now time to implement the change as approved. In the agile development world, the team simply changes the next increment it will work on, depending on the new priorities. Regardless of the methodology used, the core team continually strives to *reduce the cost of changes* and *welcomes changes that add value to the business.*

Tracing Requirements through the BSLC

A key element of requirements management is *tracing* requirements throughout system design and development to track where in the system each requirement is satisfied. As requirements are converted to design documentation, which is composed of design specification and schematics, the requirement and design documentation must be linked to ensure that the relevant business needs are satisfied. Likewise, as the solution is constructed, requirements are traced to hardware and software components, as well as to other items such as training documentation.

Allocating Requirements

Each unique requirement is allocated to a component of the solution. As the requirement is satisfied, the actual solution component that is satisfying the requirement is noted. This approach allows for ease of sorting and additional analysis to ensure that the requirement is satisfied completely. This component allocation categorization initializes the traceability mechanism for each requirement as it is allocated to system components and constructed and tested. Typical component categories for business solutions appear below. This list is not all-inclusive and is modified based on the needs of the project.

+ Software (SW)

+ Hardware (HW)

+ Infrastructure (IS)

+ Product constraint (PC)

+ Training (TR)

+ Documentation (DC)

+ Testing (TS)

Tracing Requirements

In addition to tracing requirements to the solution components, it is also helpful to link and trace dependent requirement artifacts. Suzanne Robertson and James Robertson, in their book *Mastering the Requirements Process*, present three traceability needs.[1]

+ To trace the *use case(s)* to the *business event response(s)* and vice versa. This is accomplished by assigning a unique number to each business event and to each use case and creating a connection between them.

+ To trace all *use cases* affected by a *requirement* and vice versa. This is accomplished by giving each requirement an identification number and connecting it to the relevant use cases.

+ To keep track of which requirements—or parts of requirements—are implemented by which pieces of technology (similar to the discussion above). One way of doing this is to maintain an up-to-date allocated business event-response model that is cross-referenced to solution components.

Tracing requirements is an ongoing process used to ensure that each step in the development process is correct, conforms to the needs of the prior step, and is not superfluous. Requirements tracing is an important technique in the struggle to help ensure that project teams are designing and implementing the right system. The trick is to implement just the right amount of traceability in just the right way so that the risk-to-reward ratio fits the project circumstances. Likewise, the use of tools for traceability depends on the size, risk, and complexity of the project. The most common tool for this is the requirements traceability matrix (RTM). Many commercial tools make requirements traceability simple and straightforward. On very small, low-risk projects, a spreadsheet might be an appropriate tool for the RTM. (See Appendix E, Requirements Traceability Matrix Template for Hardware, Software and Test Case Traceability.) Keeping the RTM current can be a laborious task, bogging down the team members. Keep the process as simple as possible. Remember, barely sufficient is good enough! (Refer to Figure 8-1 for a sample RTM.)

Endnote

1. Suzanne Robertson and James Robertson. *Mastering the Requirements Process*, 1999. Boston: Addison-Wesley.

Figure 8-1—Requirements Traceability Matrix

Name	Test Req ID	REQ DOC ID	REQ Ref.	Cover Status	Project Name	Author	Creation Date	App.	Priority
TEST	445	BRD 1_1_2006	REQ1.1	Not Covered	2012 I&WF	tchvet	05/17/2006	I & WF	C
test_req1	446	BRD 1_1_2006	REQ1.5	Passed	2012 I&WF	tchvet	05/17/2006	I & WF	C
test_req2	447	BRD 1_1_2006	REQ2.3	Not Covered	2012 I&WF	tchvet	05/18/2006	I & WF	H
test_req3	448	BRD 1_1_2006	REQ5.4	Not Covered	2012 I&WF	tchvet	05/18/2006	I & WF	L

Chapter 9

Analysis Best Practices

In This Chapter:

- Facilitated Workshops

- Uncovering Expectations

- Interim Reviews and Feedback

- Collaboration

- Modeling to Understand the Business

These are exciting times to be a business analyst. Not only is business analysis becoming a profession in and of itself, but also an array of powerful tools and techniques are emerging to make the business analyst successful. We present just a few here for your consideration. Use them to enhance your toolkit and gain credibility as a professional business analyst.

Facilitated Workshops

One of the most powerful tools to drive project success is professionally facilitated sessions. The process of consulting, facilitating, and scribing results for immediate feedback is one of the best techniques in the business analyst's tool kit. Collaborating with the project manager, the business analyst uncovers several opportunities to conduct a facilitated session:

- During pre-project activities, the strategic planning and enterprise analysis phases of the BSLC, the senior business analyst plays a critical role in providing information to and facilitating working sessions of the management team to establish, select, and prioritize investments in the most valuable project opportunities.

- When a project begins, facilitated planning is essential to building the foundation for project success through consensus decision making. Having all the key stakeholders participating in the launch of the project ensures a common understanding of the project. In addition, it enables the participants to collaboratively develop the overall project approach and plans. Facilitated sessions foster discovery of the issues, risks, assumptions, and constraints that the project will face. Measures of success are also developed and understood. Project schedules and milestones are developed. Through facilitated project kickoff sessions, a common understanding of the project and a commitment to the project goals and plans emerge.

- As the project moves into the requirements phase of the BSLC, the facilitated sessions grow in importance. Throughout the processes of requirements elicitation, analysis, and specification, getting the right people together is essential. Doing so delivers better results early, avoiding rework and leading to higher quality in the requirement deliverables.

Refer to another volume in the series, *The Art and Power of Facilitation: Running Powerful Meetings*, for a detailed discussion on how to plan and conduct a requirements workshop.

Uncovering Expectations

Undiscovered stakeholder expectations can be damaging to a project. By their very nature, expectations are unwritten requirements. It is not enough simply to ask stakeholders what their requirements are or to ask stakeholders to record their requirements in an RFP, statement of work (SOW), or some other format. Insist on using a set of analysis-understanding models to fully understand the business, the expectations of the stakeholders, and the intended use of the solution. The modeling techniques described in this book will go a long way in fully exposing the expectations of stakeholders. However, in many small projects or projects that have a very condensed timeframe, modeling is omitted or very limited. In such cases, it is essential to have conversations with the stakeholders to uncover their expectations. Questions like the following will help ferret out the stakeholders' expectations:

+ How do you expect to use the system?

+ How do you think it will benefit you?

+ How will you determine the success of the requirements (or project)?

+ In your mind, what is wrong with the current solution or situation?

+ What do you think is the opportunity going forward?

+ What do you think will be the barriers to implementation?

+ What is the quantifiable business value you expect from the new solution?

Interim Reviews and Feedback

Throughout the entire analysis process, there should be interim reviews and feedback loops. These reviews have a dual purpose: (1) to review the latest view of a requirement artifact, a prototype, or a component of the solution and (2) to capture lessons learned during the latest iteration. Incorporate lessons learned immediately after the review to continuously improve your analysis approach. These reviews can be simple peer reviews or formal sessions with the appropriate facilitation. Formal reviews are disciplined sessions that ensure that the requirements are valid and ready to be baselined and put under change control.

Collaboration

One of the most important elements for success when analyzing and specifying requirements is developing a collaborative working relationship between the business and technical teams. Some suggestions on how to create this collaborative environment follow:

- **Identify leaders within the business community.** Select persons that will be responsible for setting up meetings for you and will be responsible for managing communication within the business.

- **Meet regularly.** Assemble a core team of people and meet weekly to discuss the current state of the requirements, as well as potential needs going forward. Indeed, some agile teams conduct daily stand-up meetings to make decisions and course corrections in real time.

- **Learn the business.** Seek to understand the roles and responsibilities of key business partners. This will establish you as a key business expert.

- **Seek advice.** When starting a project, seek advice from all partners in the business and technical communities.

- At the risk of repeating ourselves, **seek feedback early and often.** When analyzing the scope, analyzing the business, or specifying the requirements, seek feedback from all stakeholders throughout the process.

✦ **Create a knowledge base.** Document the group's learning and approach in developing business requirements. As you conduct lessons learned sessions often throughout the effort on all requirements development projects, regardless of size, document and incorporate the learning into the next requirements process.

Modeling to Understand the Business

Because organizations are now beginning to use modeling extensively, lessons are emerging. The summary of modeling best practices below is based on the work of Scott Ambler.[1]

✦ Modeling is a collaborative activity. Include both business and technical SMEs in your modeling sessions.

✦ Keep models as simple as possible. Do not drive too far into the details. Continue building models until you have a basic understanding of the high-level requirements and a potential architectural solution is emerging. Remember the agile maxim: barely sufficient is enough to move on.

✦ Use the simplest technology that will do the job. For example, use a Visio diagram instead of a CASE tool model if the Visio model will suffice.

✦ Try to move as quickly as possible to prototyping or component building to validate requirements. If you spend too much time modeling, you delay receiving feedback on the solution components themselves. A model might work quite well on paper but might not be suitable for the solution during the construction phases.

✦ Model with a purpose so that when the purpose is met, you know you are finished.

+ If you get stuck, stop modeling and go on to something else.

+ Build smaller requirements into artifacts like user stories or features. These are much easier to estimate, manage, and build than are larger requirements like use cases.

+ Do not capture the same information in more than one place.

The common modeling challenges below are also based on Ambler's work.[2] Project teams must strive to overcome the following challenges to successfully incorporating modeling into their business solution life cycle:

+ Limited access to project stakeholders

+ Geographically dispersed project stakeholders

+ Project stakeholders that do not know what they want

+ Project stakeholders that change their minds

+ Conflicting priorities

+ Too many project stakeholders that want to participate

+ Project stakeholders that prescribe technology solutions

+ Project stakeholders that are unable to see beyond the current situation

+ Project stakeholders that are afraid to be pinned down

+ Project stakeholders that don't understand modeling artifacts

+ Developers that don't understand the problem domain

+ Project stakeholders that are overly focused on one type of requirement

- Project stakeholders that require significant formality regarding requirements

- Developers that don't understand the requirements.

Endnotes

1. Scott Ambler. *Agile Requirements Best Practices.* Online at http://www.agilemodeling.com/essays/agileRequirementsBestPractices.htm (accessed August 2006).

2. Scott Ambler. *Overcoming Requirements Modeling Challenges.* Online at http://www.agilemodeling.com/essays/requirementsChallenges.htm (accessed August 21, 2006).

Chapter 10

The Business Analyst's Toolbox: Selecting the Right Requirements Analysis Techniques

By Kevin Brennan

In This Chapter:

- Enterprise Architecture

- The Business Analyst Role

- Model Coverage

Over the last few decades, the business consulting and software development communities have developed a bewildering array of different business analysis techniques to understand and describe processes, policies, and systems. As a practical matter, a business analyst is never going to have the time or need to become a skilled practitioner of all of these techniques.

While you can leave the techniques you'll study up to the discretion of the organization for which you work, how will you know if your skills are portable? How can you be sure that you've mastered enough techniques to handle new situations that might arise? Fortunately, a business analyst can usually manage with only a small set of carefully chosen techniques, as long as he or she picks the right set of complementary analysis methods.

Figuring out which techniques to learn can be tricky, however. Most contemporary methodologies aspire to provide coverage for a complete solution development lifecycle, but they may not address things that fall outside the approach envisioned by the method's creators. Other resources, like the *Guide to the Business Analysis Body of Knowledge (BABOK™)*, are comprehensive but not prescriptive, as they strive to be methodology neutral.

Enterprise Architecture

An enterprise architecture is intended to provide guidance to an organization as to what sorts of processes are needed to support on-going systems development and change improvement efforts. (See *The Business Analyst as Strategist: Translating Business Strategies into Valuable Solutions*, another book in this series, for a detailed discussion of enterprise architecture.) An enterprise architecture framework helps organizations address everything from strategic planning to application maintenance and operational support. By definition, then, everything a business analyst does should fit into the enterprise architecture adopted by an organization. If you know enough different analysis techniques to cover the breadth of an enterprise framework, you know enough to address almost any conceivable situation or project that might arise.

The Zachman Framework[1] is one of several models for the development of an enterprise architecture. It focuses on documenting different perspectives of an organization, which makes it easy to show which analysis techniques can be used to describe specific cells in the framework. However, if you work in an organization that has adopted a different architecture framework, the lessons should still apply. (See *The Business Analyst as Strategist* for a detailed discussion of the Zachman Framework.) The Zachman Framework takes the six classic questions (who, what, where, why, when, and how) and describes the models required to answer those questions in the context of a particular organization. For example, "how?" translates to "how does this organization do things?"

The framework then defines six different levels of abstraction for the answers to each question. At the top level, we define the overall scope of the business—what processes, people, and events exist that are of interest to us. The second level, the business model, looks at how all those things of interest relate to each other and interact with one another. Below that there's a system model, which describes in detail what each of those things is. This continues down until we have the actual applications, data, and so forth.

Not all of the levels of the Zachman Framework are relevant to a person in the business analysis role, since the business analyst focuses on the *business architecture* and leaves the remaining elements to the technical team to define. When we look at the scope of the *BABOK*™, we find that business analysts generally work down as far as the system model, but will in some cases go a little deeper. Figure 10-1 shows how the Zachman Framework maps to the range of activities found in the *BABOK*™. The gray cells in this picture indicate cells that fall outside of the scope of the business analyst role.

The Business Analyst Role

If you count, you'll see that the BA has a role to play in filling in 21 of 36 cells in the framework. That sounds like a lot, I know. However, 21 different techniques are not required to describe all those models. In practice, you should need to master no more than six or seven—one for every column in the framework. That's because most analysis techniques are intended to operate at multiple levels of abstraction, and also because many techniques cover the same columns. The following discussion provides a brief description of the models used to answer the classic questions about an organization.

Figure 10-1—General Scope of Business Analysis Activities in the Zachman Framework

	Data (What)	Function (How)	Network (Where)	People (Who)	Time (When)	Motivation (Why)
Scope (Level 1)	Entity	Process List	Locations of the Enterprise	List of Organizations/Divisions	Major Business Events or Cycles	Business Strategy
Business Model (Level 2)	Entity/Relationship	Overall Process Model	Interactions Between Locations	Organization Chart, List of Roles	Detailed Schedule	Business Plan, Project Objectives
System Model (Level 3)	Logical Data Model	Detailed Process Description		Detailed Interaction Model	Entity History, Processing	Business Rule Model
Technology Model (Level 4)				User Interface Design and Flow		Business Rule Specification
Detailed Representation (Level 5)				Detailed UI, Security		Business Rule Design
Functioning Enterprise (Level 6)						

- **Data** models focus on describing what the business knows about things of interest and the relationships that those things have to one another.

- **Function** models describe how the business gets things done and how the business works to achieve its goals. A function model will generally involve multiple people over a period of time—work that can be done by a single person in a single sitting is covered by people models.

- **Network** models describe where the enterprise does work and how work performed at different locations is integrated. Of all of the columns, this one is probably the least important to the typical BA—as the name suggests, the people in IT who it concerns most are the network support personnel.

- **People** models tell you who is of concern to the solution. In many cases, this model is nothing more than a stakeholder definition, but for commercial products, it may include things like a market segmentation. At lower levels, people models describe how stakeholders interact with a solution to accomplish their personal goals and responsibilities through the user interface.

- **Time** models describe when events happen and when events can happen. A time model does not cover sequencing (that's a function) but rather expresses regular cycles that the business has to go through (like tax filing) or events that require a response.

- **Motivation** models describe how the business makes decisions and why those decisions are made. A policy model describes who may make a decision, the information that they use to make that decision, and the rules that guide them in making that decision.

Model Coverage

Figure 10-2 shows which requirements types can be expressed by which common (and a couple of less common) business analysis techniques. Obviously, these techniques have strengths and weaknesses that will not be obvious from just looking at the chart below—but the chart does tell you when a technique *can* be used to do.

So how does this help a business analyst figure out which techniques to master? By now it should be obvious—you should be able to use at least one primary technique for each column in the Zachman Framework, and consider learning secondary techniques as and where required. You may find that text or matrices will suffice for describing some requirements (for instance, motivation requirements, especially the higher level ones, are often described in a business case or vision document).

The particular techniques you choose to learn will depend on the business domain you work in, the methodologies chosen by your organization, and other considerations. Not every project requires that you be able to completely describe all possible kinds of requirements. On the other hand, if you work intensively in a particular cell of the framework, you may want to be familiar with more than one technique that applies to it for use with different audiences or to resolve different issues.

When the time comes to handle a new problem, though, you should now have the tools you need to figure out whether something you already know how to do will help you solve it—or whether learning something new is going to be necessary.

Figure 10-2—Specific Analysis Techniques and the Zachman Framework

Technique	Data	Function	Network	Time	People	Motivation
Activity Diagram		2,3		•	3	
Business Process/Workflow Diagram	•	1,2,3			3	•
Business Rules	•	•				3,4,5
Class Model	1,2,3				5	4,5
CRUD Matrix	•					
Data Dictionary	3					
Data Flow Diagram	•	1,2,3	•		•	•
Data Transformation and Mapping	•					
Deployment Diagram			1,2			
Entity Relationship Diagrams	1,2,3		•			
Event Identification		•		1,2		•
Flowchart		2,3			3,4	
i*/Goal-oriented Requirements Language					•	1,2,3
Metadata Definition	•			•	•	
Sequence Diagram	•			3	5	
State Machine Diagram	•			1,2,3	•	
Storyboards/Screen Flows		1,2,3			3,4,5	
Use Cases				•	2,3,4	•
User Interface Designs					3,4,5	
User Profiles					1,2	•
User Stories		•			•	•

Legend 1, 2, 3, 4, 5 Framework level that the technique addresses
        • Indicates that the technique can capture these requirements but is not optimized for that purpose.

Endnotes

1. John A. Zachman. *The Zachman Framework for Enterprise Architecture.* Pinckney, MI: The Zachman Institute for Framework Advancement. Online at http://www.zifa.com/ (accessed August 9, 2007).

Appendixes

Appendix A:
Stakeholder Analysis Template

Appendix B:
Requirements Management Plan Template

Appendix C:
Communication Plan Template

Appendix D:
Business Requirements Document Template

Appendix E:
Requirements Traceability Matrix Template

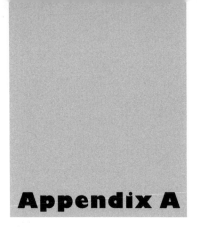

Appendix A

Stakeholder Analysis Template

Stakeholder Interest and Impact Table

Stakeholder	Interests	Influence	Importance	Estimated Priority
Business Unit Manager	Achieve Targets	Medium	Medium	2
Sponsor	Provide New Market	High	High	1
CFO	Reduce Costs	High	High	1

Stakeholder Importance—Influence classification

Conduct a formal assessment of each stakeholder's level of importance and influence to the project.

+ Influence indicates the stakeholder's relative power over and within the project.

+ Importance indicates the degree to which the project cannot be considered successful if needs, expectations, and issues are not addressed.

Consider the relationship of the stakeholder to the project's goals and purposes.

The project, for example, may have an important financial sponsor who can shut the project down at any time for any reason but who rarely participates.

Consider diagramming the relationships to understand potential risks and highlight groups of stakeholders whose needs can be addressed in a common manner. Use a range of numbers (0–10) or high, medium, and low. The stakeholders in the high influence–high importance quadrant are key stakeholders. However, those in the low importance–high influence quadrant have the potential to become a high project risk as well. For example, someone who does not have any apparent needs or provides no technical requirements to the project but who has undue influence over a key funding source should be monitored carefully.

Appendix B

Requirements Management Plan Template

Logo

Organization Name

Project Title

Requirements Management Plan (RMP)

Draft Version: 1.0

Date Prepared:

Prepared by:

Table of Contents

Document Information

Revision History

Version	Date	Author(s)	Revision Notes

Approval

The signatures below confirm that this document has been reviewed and is complete and accurate for the project.

Team Member	Signature	
		Date
		Date
		Date
		Date
		Date
		Date
		Date

1.0 Introduction

Overview of Scope

Describe the purpose, scope, and objectives of the document.

This document describes the guidelines used by the project for eliciting, analyzing, specifying, documenting, and validating the business requirements. In addition, it describes the process to be used for requirement traceability and change management. This document is a subsidiary element of the overall project plan.

Overview of Requirements Standards

Provide an overview of the organizational standards, how they have been tailored for this project, and any additional project-specific guidelines and expectations.

Related Documents

List all related documents, such as program documents, test plans, glossaries, standard operating procedures/work instructions. For existing documents, provide author, issue date, and storage location of the electronic version. Potential examples include:

+ Business Case Document [insert author, date, and location]

+ Business Requirements Document [insert author, date, and location]

+ Supplementary Requirements Specification [insert author, date, and location]

2.0 Stakeholders

List the stakeholders that are involved in the requirements definition and management process.

This is a listing of the stakeholders that will be involved in requirements gathering, documenting, and management. This is not an exhaustive project stakeholder analysis, but is meant to provide the preliminary information needed to begin the requirements elicitation activities. It will also contribute to the overall stakeholder analysis completed by the project manager.

Stakeholder Name	Stakeholder Role/Job Title	Description of Why Project Requires Their Input or Knowledge	Degree of Influence	Required Project Involvement

Open Stakeholder Issues:

- *Sample: Lack of agreement on product champion role*

Open Stakeholder Risks:

- *Sample: Lack of access to stakeholders for business requirements*

3.0 Users

List end-users that are involved in the requirements management process.

This is a listing of the end-user groups that will be involved in the project. This is not an exhaustive user stakeholder analysis, but is meant to provide the preliminary information needed to begin the requirements elicitation activities. It will also contribute to the overall stakeholder analysis completed by the project manager.

User Group Name	User Roles	Domain Expertise	Technology Expertise	User Group Priority

Open User Involvement Issues:

- *Sample: Lack of funding to cover all user classes*

Open User Involvement Risks:

- *Sample: Lack of access to users for use case development*

4.0 Requirement Deliverables

4.1 Documents and Models

List the requirement documents, deliverables, and other artifacts that will be created by the project team. Examples of requirement artifacts appear below; this is not meant to be an exhaustive list.

The following requirement artifacts are required for this project.

Document Name	Requirements Type(s)	Description
Business requirements document	Functional	Capability desired by the customer.
	Assumptions	Something assumed to be real, true or certain for the project.
	Constraints	A project limitation.
	Glossary	Defines important terms used by project stakeholders. Terms are defined in natural (non-technical) language.
	Design constraints	A design limitation. Content most often provided by the technical design team.
	Business rules	An agreed-upon business procedure that leads to a decision on how to respond to a condition. Content most often provided by customers and users.
Use case and any other usage, process or high-level data model	Functional	Provides high-level view of all Use-Cases and Actors (or indicate elements for each analysis model required) for this release documented in xxx vendor application. Content provided by customers and users.
Supplementary requirements document	Supplemental	Provides non-feature-related information.
Requirements traceability matrix	Functional	Captures the allocation of functional requirements to system components, e.g., design specifications, program modules, test case, etc.
Design specification	n/a	Contains the design elements and architecture for the proposed business solution.
Test plan	n/a	Contains the strategy for testing coverage within the project.

Test case	n/a	A specific set of test inputs, environmental conditions, and expected results developed for a particular objective.

4.2 Attributes

Separately list the information that is required when specifying requirements. Sample information required appears below; this is not meant to be an exhaustive list.

The following is a list, by requirement type, of the required information that must be captured for each type of artifact.

Requirement Attributes for Functional Requirements

+ # (unique identifier)

+ Status

+ Benefit/business value (quantified or high/medium/low)

+ Effort (quantified or high/medium/low)

+ Description

+ Rationale

+ Source

+ Event/use case number

+ Supporting materials/documents

+ Dependencies (required whether manual or automated system)

+ Change history (this may be unnecessary if requirements are managed by an automated application)

+ Priority (based on business value)

Requirement Attributes for Supplemental Requirements

+ Effort (quantified or high/medium/low)

Requirement Attributes for Actors

+ Name and brief description of role

Requirement Attributes for Use Cases

+ Name

+ Brief description

+ Basic flow

+ Alternate flow

+ Special requirements

+ Pre-condition

+ Post-condition

5.0 Verification and Validation Processes

Allocation Process

Describe the requirement allocation process.

Traceability Process

Describe the requirements traceability process.

Peer Review Process

Describe the peer review process.

Customer Review Process

Describe the process and participants for the customer review process.

Management Review Process

Describe the process and participants for the management review process, including the requirements phase-exit control gate review.

6.0 Change Management Processes

Change Management Process

Describe the requirements change management process.

7.0 Risk Management

Describe the requirement risk identification, assessment, and risk response planning process.

Note: the requirement risk management process is provided to the project manager for further incorporation into the overall project risk management plan.

8.0 Deliverables Owners, Dependencies, and Resource Estimates

Provide project planning detail for all the artifacts to be created to manage requirements. Note: this list should include all deliverables listed in Section 4.0. Examples of requirement artifacts appear below; this is not meant to be an exhaustive list.

The requirements deliverables, ownership, and project planning information are as follows.

Requirements Development Artifacts

Key Deliverables	Owner	Time Est.	Dependency	Template	Comments / Risks / Issues
Requirements Management Plan Document	BA	x hours	Business Case and Charter	RMP.dot	No organizational template exists which could delay approval since there is not agreement on content
Committed Stakeholders	BA/PM	n/a	none	na	Need donor user representative to confirm understanding of the use cases
Elicitation Phase					
Requirements Workshop	BA	24 hours	Approved Requirements Management Plan		Estimate may need to be doubled as we need additional training or facilitation help in this area
Analysis Phase					
Context Diagram	BA	x hours	High-Level Product Description	ContextDiagram.dot	Accounting doesn't want any changes but it is a required interface
User Classes & Goals	BA	x hours	Stakeholder analysis	Usergoals.dot	Need product champions for each user class
Prioritization of Use Cases	BA	x hours	User Classes & Goals	n/a – see User Classes & Goals	
Use Case Diagram	BA	n/a			None – will use User Class list since small number of use cases
Use Case Scenarios	BA	60 hours	UC Diagram	Usecase.dot UCDefectList.dot	The organization has not used these before and so there is training involved
Validation Phase					
Prototypes	TL/BA	60 hours	Use Case Scenarios	n/a	Need a user product champion and a dedicated resource from accounting

Key Deliverables	Owner	Time Est.	Dependency	Template	Comments / Risks / Issues
Feasibility Studies/ Reliability Studies	BA	n/a	Draft BRD		Create an RFP from the BRD to research availability and feature sets of COTS applications
Documentation Phase					
Project Summary	PM	x hours	Business Case and Charter	Charter.dot	Missing charter
Business Requirements Document	BA	n/a	Elicitation & draft Analysis models complete	Yes	Choose to create only Use Cases and Supplementary Business Requirements
Supplemental Business Requirements	BA/SA	24 hours	Draft BRD	SBR.dot SBRDefectList.dot	Organization has not agreed on a template or organizational standards
Glossary	BA	4 hours	Use Case Scenarios	n/a	There isn't an existing glossary so only critical terms will be documented

Requirements Management Artifacts

Key Deliverables	Owner-ship	Time *	Dependency	Template	Comments / Risks / Issues
Requirements Traceability Matrix	BA/SA	TBD	Decision on tool purchase	TBD	Will provide time estimate before requirements phase gate
Test Plan	Test Manager/BA	TBD	BRD, Use Cases, Supplement Business Requirements	TBD	Will provide time estimate before requirements phase gate
Requirements Change Management Process	PM/BA	TBD	Decision on tool purchase PM to create process	TBD	Will provide time estimate before requirements phase gate

*Note: This may not the final time estimate for the requirements activities that will be used in the project schedule, but is useful for making project trade-off decisions on which activities to include in the final project schedule.

Environmental Needs and Responsibilities

Provide details of any special environment set-up needs. This section covers office space, equipment needs, and software tool needs. Resources may be available within the organization but need to be identified for scheduling and chargebacks.

The environmental needs for the project are as follows.

Deliverable	Description	Owner

Training

Provide details of training required for all core and extended team members to accomplish the requirement activities.

The training needs for the project are as follows.

Resource Type	Training Need, Timing, and Cost	Functional Manager/Owner Commitments (y/n)

Requirements Schedule

Provide the milestone schedule commitments to be used in overall project planning.

The requirements milestones and schedule for the project are as follows.

Milestone	Due Date

9.0 Glossary

Define key requirements terms to be included in the overall project glossary. Define terms in natural, nontechnical language.

Key requirements terms

- Key term 1—explanation of term

Appendix C

Communication Plan Template

[Project Name]

Communication Plan

Draft Version:

Date Prepared:

Prepared by:

Document Control

Document Information

	Information
Document ID	
Document Owner	
Issue Date	

Document History

Version	Issue Date	Changes

Table of Contents

Communications Plan

1   Communications Approach

    1.1   Goals

    1.2   Communication Strategies

    1.3   Related Documents

2   Communications Plan

    2.1   Schedule for Communications [next page]

3   Assumptions and Risks

    3.1   Assumptions

    3.2   Risks

Schedule for Communications

ID	Event	Description	Purpose	Measure of Success	Method	Frequency	Date(s)	Owner

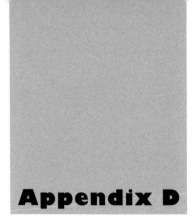

Appendix D

Business Requirements Document Template

Organization Name

Project Title

Business Requirements Document (BRD)

Draft Version: 1.0

Date Prepared:

Prepared by:

Table of Contents

Document Information

Revision History

Version	Date	Author(s)	Revision Notes

Approval

The signatures below confirm that this document has been reviewed and is complete and accurate for the project.

Senior Management and Project Team Leads	Signature	
		Date
		Date
		Date
		Date
		Date
		Date
		Date

1.0 Introduction

Purpose

Describe the project scope and the phase to which this project applies.

This business requirements document (BRD) describes the requirements for release 1.0 of the (*insert solution, system or project name here*). This document is for use by the members of the project team that will design, construct and verify the system or process and by the customer to confirm that this solution will satisfy their needs.

Project Scope

Provide an overview of the organization or project standards, guidelines and expectations.

The (*insert solution, system or project name here*) will provide (*organization name*) with the following business and high level feature requirements. This document represents the scope of the project. If a feature is included, it is assumed to be of high priority and included in this release.
Describe the solution in high-level textual terms.

Project Client

Provide the name of the sponsor or the client.

Provide the funding source and name. Describe any background information on the project approval or release of funds to the project.

Project Budget

Provide an overview of the budget constraints and the source of the constraint.

The budget for this system is not to exceed ($x), including hardware, software capital equipment, expensed equipment or license purchases.

Project Schedule

Provide an overview of the schedule constraints and the source of the constraints.

The system must be complete within (*insert constraint here*) months but does not need to include all the (*list follow-up phase features or lower priority features here*).

Related Documents

List all documents that exist relating to this project, such as: program documents, document and model templates, defect check lists, glossaries, and standard operating procedures/work instructions. Also list any current system document that was used to describe the as-is process or was used in re-engineering solutions.

Examples:
1. Business Case (Location or URL)
2. Charter (Location or URL)
3. Supplemental Business Requirements (Location or URL)
4. Use Cases (Location or URL)

2.0 Project Stakeholders

Stakeholder Summary

List the results of the stakeholder analysis completed by the project manager. Identify how representative stakeholders were involved in the requirements discovery (pre-project) process. State how conflicts in stakeholder group interests were resolved.

3.0 Overall Description

Business Need

This describes a high- level summary if the reason that this project was undertaken and the phase to which this project applies (if applicable). Use natural, non-technical language. The intended audience is either the customer or senior management.

The (*insert solution, system or project name here*) is a new system or process that replaces the current manual processes for (*continue to provide a high-level business overview of the need*).

Business Solution Overview/Problem Domain Model or Business Process Model

This provides a high-level summary of the business solution described in this document. The intended audience is either the customer or senior management. It may be necessary to provide a graphical representation of a high-level business solution describing system boundaries or major components. Give a description of the major components of the system.

An example is a use case diagram serving as the problem domain model. This represents scope of the business solution at a high level. It identifies actors and events outside the system that interact with it, without describing internal structure. A problem domain model may look like the following:

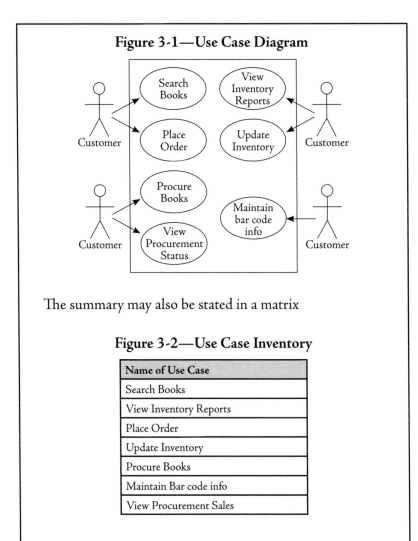

Figure 3-1—Use Case Diagram

The summary may also be stated in a matrix

Figure 3-2—Use Case Inventory

Name of Use Case
Search Books
View Inventory Reports
Place Order
Update Inventory
Procure Books
Maintain Bar code info
View Procurement Sales

Approaches

State the recommended and alternative approaches to solve the business need. The intended audience is either the customer or senior management.

♦

♦

Metrics

Discuss the business metrics that will be improved by the implementation of the solution in specific and measurable terms.

+

+

Assumptions

Project assumptions clarify gray areas in the project. List any known assumptions or special requirements that have been made regarding the project that may influence this agreement should be noted in the table below. Assumptions are made to fill knowledge gaps; they may later prove to be incorrect and can have a significant impact on the project.

+

+

Constraints

Any known constraints imposed by the environment or by management should be noted. Typical constraints may include: fixed budget, limited resources, imposed interim and/or end dates, predetermined software systems and packages and other predetermined solutions

+

+

4.0 User Summary

User Summary

Provide the user analysis completed by the business analyst. Identify how representative users were involved in the requirements discovery process. State how conflicts in user needs were resolved.

Users of the Product/Process

List the user names, roles and their domain knowledge expertise and their technology experience. Describe any other relevant information that impacts requirements. List the prioritization of the users groups. List the user participation in the requirements elicitation, analysis, specification, validation and documentation processes.

User environment

Describe how the user environment impacts the requirements.

User Classes and Goals

Insert the completed table here. This provides additional information on the high-level commitments made in the use case inventory listed above.

Figure 4-1—Actor Goals

Primary Actor/User		Use Case Goals/Feature Goals
Donor	1	Give Donation
	2	
	3	
	4	
	5	
	6	
	7	
	8	
	9	
	10	

5.0 Functional Requirements

Feature Description

Describe the business solution behavior requested by the users.

The following are sample business scenarios that are included in the first release of the Donation Tracking system.

1.1. Give donations

1.1.1. As-Is

An individual donation is either received over the phone or in the mail. This information is written down on a donor form if received over the phone. Only actual donation information is entered into the accounting system. Fields are not verified for accuracy.

1.1.2. To-Be Description and Priority

An individual donor who is verified to have information listed in the Fundraising Tracking System will be able to provide payment information. An individual donor may change the donation amount, change the donation payment method or cancel their donation. This must be in the first release of the project.

1.1.3. To-Be Stimulus/Response Sequences

Stimulus: Donor agrees to provide a donation
Response: Phone rep asks donor for details of the payment

Stimulus: Donor requests a change in donation amount
Response: If donation amount is found, system allows phone rep to modify a previous donation amount.

Stimulus: Donor requests a cancellation of a donation amount

Response: If donation amount is found, system allows phone rep to cancel a previous donation amount.

1.1.4. To-Be Give Donations Functional Requirements

Donation.Place:	The system will let a phone rep who is logged into the Fundraising Tracking System enter one or more donations
Donation.Place.Record:	The system shall confirm that the donor has an information record in the system.
Donation.Place.Record.No:	If the donor is not listed in the system, the system will collect the information needed to continue with the donation process.
Donation.Place.Date:	The system shall prompt the phone rep for the donation date.
Donation.Gift.Select:	The system shall prompt the phone rep to offer gifts to donors (see BR**)
Donation.Pay.Methods:	When the donor is done providing donations and selecting a gift, the system shall ask for a payment method.

Donation.Done:	When the donor has confirmed the donation, the system shall do the following as a single transaction:
Donation.Done.Store:	Assign the next available donation number to the donation with an initial status of "accepted."
Donation.Done.Ship:	Send a message to the shipping clerk to send the selected gift.
Donation.Done.Donor:	Send a message to the Patron with the donation number and the payment information.
Donation.Done.Accounting:	Send a message to the accounting system with the donation information.
Donation.Done.Failure:	If any step of the Donation. Done fails, the system shall roll back the transaction and notify the donor that the donation payment was unsuccessful, along with the reason for the failure.

(Functional requirements for changing and canceling donations are not provided in this example.)

1.2. Register for email newsletter
TBD

1.3. Create, View, Modify and Delete Marketing Content
TBD

1.4. Report Requirements (Ad-hoc and Scheduled)
TBD

Risks

Any future events that if they occur will positively or negatively impact the project.

- ◆

- ◆

Open and Closed Issues

Item	Date	Who Raised issue?	Urgency	Description of Issue or Action Item	Closed	Comments
1						
2						
3						

6.0 Supplemental Requirements

Describe the supplemental requirements required by the users.

The following are sample supplemental requirements.

1. **Access Management Requirements**
1.1. **Roles and Permissions**
    1.1.1.   Describe, at a conceptual level, who will have access to the system or its components and what type of access they will have
1.2. **System Impacts**

2. **External Interface Requirements**
2.1. **Usability Requirements**
    2.1.1.   The Fundraising Tracking System will provide help links to explain usage of each page.
    2.1.2.   Wireframes (available before requirements phase exit)
    2.1.3.   Field-level descriptions (available in design phase)
2.2. **Hardware Interfaces**
    2.2.1.   TBD
2.3. **Software Interfaces**
    2.3.1.   The Assistance Inc. accounting systems
    2.3.1.1. To allow a phone rep to check whether there is a record for a donor on file
    2.3.1.2. To transit new donor name and address information
    2.3.1.3. To update donor name and address information
    2.3.1.4. To transmit the donation amount
    2.3.1.5. To change or cancel the donation amount

2.4 Communications Interfaces

2.4.1. The FTS shall send shipping an email message to send a gift to a donor

2.4.2. The FTS shall send donor an email message to a donor for a donation commitment

2.4.3. The FTS shall send donor an email message to a donor for a donation acknowledge and details of the donation payment.

2.4.4. The FTS shall send donor an email message for a donation payment failure.

3. Security Requirements

3.1. Specify in business language the security or privacy constraints that the system must respect or adhere too.

4. Performance Requirements

4.1. State in business terms user or system requirements that designers need to consider.

5. Software Quality Attributes

5.1. State the product quality characteristics that are important to stakeholders. Some to consider are maintainability, supportability, interoperability, availability (if not covered under performance).

6. Business Rules

6.1. An agreed-upon procedure, guideline, regulation or standard that leads to a decision on how a system should to respond to a condition. Business rules document the policies that the business must follow. These rules may be documented as text, or created as a matrix of conditions and business solution responses. These are not functional requirements in themselves, but they may require functional requirements to execute the rules.

Appendix A: Glossary

Key requirements terms

Defines key requirements terms and acronyms

- •
- •

Appendix B: Use Cases

List high-level use case information (further information will be provided in the requirements phase as each iteration of the use cases are completed).

Case #	Feature	Business Requirement	Actors	Pre-Condition	Post-Condition
1	Give Donation				
2	Change Donation				
3	Cancel Donation				

A sample use case is provided below.

B-1 Give Donation

1. Description

An internal user enters information provided by a donor into the Fundraising Tracking System (FTS).

2. Actors

1. FTS Users
2. FTS
3. Security Management (SM) API

3. Pre-conditions

1. Donor has an existing record
2. User access to FTS Give Donation function in SM API

4. Basic Flow

Step	Description
1	The use case begins when a user wants to enter donation information.
2	The user logs in.
3	The system grants access to the Donations screen according the permissions on SM matrix.
4	The system searches for donor information. *(Alt Course A: Can not find existing donor)* *(Alt Course B: New Donor)*
5	The system excludes donors that are corporate grant partners.
6	The system displays a list of eligible last names, their first names and address. *(Exception Course A: Corporate donors are not displayed)*
7	User selects the displayed user that matches information provided by the donor. *(Exception Course B: Donor chooses not to continue with the donation process)*
8	The system displays the new donation form and the user enters the information.
9	The use case ends when the user has entered donation information.

5. Alternative Flow

Step	Description
Alt A	The system searches for donor information.
4	The system can not find any donor information. User can navigate back to the initial donations screen to enter alternative spellings.
Alt B	The user creates a new donor record.
4	The system allows the user to enter new donor information.

6. Exception Flow

Step	Description
Exp A	The system displays a list of eligible last names, their first names and address.
6	The system excludes corporate grant donors.
Exp B	User selects the displayed user that matches information provided by the donor.
7	The donor or user chooses to exit the transaction. Information is not saved.

7. Post-conditions
1. Successful transaction screen displayed
2. Donation posted to accounting
3. Credit card charged

Appendix C: Business Solution Cost Estimating

Project Hardware

Describe the hardware that is available or needs to be purchased for the project development. Describe what networks are available for possible use for the project. If the hardware platform is to be purchased then a technical architecture describing what is necessary should be documented.

Project Software

Describe the application and system software that is available or needs to be purchased for the project development.

IT Operations Impact

Describe at a high-level the hardware and software required for operational locations at which the application will be used. Provide a assumptions for hardware/software, cabling, and connectivity purchases. Describe headcount required to administer or operate the hardware/software purchased.

Business Operations Impact

Describe at a high-level the resources, facilities, training, desktop tools, servers, printers, etc. required for operational locations at which the application will be used. Describe the organizational requirements (new organizational structures, new capabilities, training, etc.) to operate business solution.

Appendix E

Requirements Traceability Matrix Template

Requirements—Design Element Traceability Matrix

	Element							
Requirement	Module S1	Module S2	Module S3	Hardware H1	Hardware H2	Hardware H3	Network N1	Network N2
1	X			X			X	
2	X			X				X
3	X	X			X			
4		X				X		
5		X		X				
6			X				X	
7			X					X

This matrix shows the relationship between requirements and the design elements (software, hardware, network) to which each requirement has been allocated.

Requirements—Test Case Traceability Matrix

	Test Case							
Requirement	Test 1.1	Test 1.2	Test 1.3	Test 2.1	Test 2.2	Test 2.3	Test 3.1	Test 4.1
1	X			X			X	
2	X			X				X
3	X	X			X			
4		X				X		
5		X		X				
6			X				X	
7			X					X

This matrix shows the relationship between requirements and the test cases that specifically test some aspect of each requirement.

Index

characteristics
   of good requirements, 102–104
collaboration
   with business and technical teams,
      124–125
communication plan
   example, 159–163
communication requirements, 35
complexity
   as challenge, 7
constraints, 89, 91–92
context diagram, 21, 46, 47, 50
   example, 51
core team, 14–16
   desired characteristics, 14–15
   roles and responsibilities, 15–16

D

data management, 16–17
data models, 63–64
deriving requirements, 8, 92–95

E

elicitation
   and requirements planning, 12
   and stakeholders, 11
   documentation review, 20–22
   requirements, 19–20
elicitation phase, 10–12
enterprise architecture, 130–131
event table, 79
event–response models, 78–79
expectations, 122–123

F

feedback, 123–124
focusing requirements, 94
functional process map
   example, 68
functional requirements, 89–90

G

gap (in modeling), 44
geographical map, 78
guidebook, 56

H

hierarchical decomposition diagrams,
   78

I

INCOSE. *See* International Council
   on System Engineering
infrastructure, 13–17
   establishing the analysis team,
      13–15
in-scope, out-of-scope list, 46, 48–49
International Council on Systems
   Engineering, 17
interpreting requirements, 93–94

L

lessons learned, 36–37
location models, 78

M

model
   technology, example, 81–82
model coverage, 134
model, application, example, 80
model, business, 44–47
modeling
   best practices, 125–127
   requirements, 7
models, 8–10, 25–27
   application, 79
   business data, 63–64
   business motivation, 79, 83
   business process, 64–67
   event–response, 78–79
   location, 78